The Light of the World

A spiritual focus for personal or group use

A 31-DAY ADVENT GUIDE

BERYL ADAMSBAUM

Published 2009 by CWR, Waverley Abbey House, Waverley Lane, Farnham, Surrey GU9 8EP, UK.
Registered Charity No. 294387. Registered Limited Company No. 1990308.

See back of book for list of National Distributors.

Unless otherwise indicated, all Scripture references are from the Holy Bible: New International
Version (NIV), copyright © 1973, 1978, 1984 by the International Bible Society.

Concept development, editing, design and production by CWR

Cover image: Getty Images/Stockbyte/Noel Hendrickson

Printed in Finland by WS Bookwell

ISBN: 978-1-85345-525-4

Contents

A Tribute

As I came to the end of writing this Advent book, my sister's husband Bill came to the end of his life. Darkness and light, the theme of this book, was also the theme chosen by Bill's son-in-law who conducted the funeral service. In a sensitive and inspiring message, he first of all recalled Bill's younger days down the mines in South Wales. Using a miner's lamp as a visual aid, he pointed out the need for a light to shine in the thick darkness of the mine. Later, as a youth worker, Bill was himself a light to the young people he worked with. More recently, he went through dark times due to the effects of cancer in his body. Concluding his message, the speaker pointed us to Jesus, whose words we have quoted in this book and which we pray will have deep personal significance for those who attended Bill's funeral: 'I am the light of the world. Whoever follows me will never walk in darkness, but will have the light of life' (John 8:12).

Introduction

Whether or not we are used to observing Advent as such, the run-up to Christmas leaves us in no doubt that something is going on! Candles, stars, lights, decorations, Christmas trees, the Nativity scene, Christmas songs and carols, and the occasional 'red-nosed reindeer', all point to a special celebration, not forgetting a sudden profusion of men with white beards, all wearing red! For some people the occasion amounts to little more than a good meal, an exchange of presents and a few days off work. Shops overflow with goods and buyers. We are all conscious of the commercialisation of Christmas.

However, I'd like us to focus on the event that took place over 2,000 years ago, which was the fulfilment of prophecy and which is our reason for celebrating. The coming of the Messiah – or the birth of Jesus Christ – had been foretold throughout the ages. In this Advent book we shall look more closely at some of those prophecies and at the state of the world – the darkness – in which people found themselves when the announcement of the coming of a Saviour resounded loud and clear amid the ambient gloom and pessimism.

The world was in darkness in Old Testament times. The world was in darkness when Jesus was born. We shall be looking in a little more detail at these periods of history as we work through this Advent book. And what about the twenty-first-century world? We are all aware of the ecological problem that we call global warming or climate change which threatens different species of animals and birds and causes damage to the earth's surface. Floods and drought cause devastation over large areas. Earthquakes seem to be on the increase, leaving thousands homeless and bereaved. And the credit crunch is a global phenomenon, causing great hardship to many and casting gloom over the earth. Wars are raging in certain parts. In some countries whole populations lack the basic necessities of life. Some are AIDS victims; others are slaves to alcohol or drugs. Add to that the moral climate – dishonesty, cheating, robbery, murder, genocide, pornography, prostitution, paedophilia … There is also piracy and persecution, and terrorism that leads to chaos and confusion and claims the lives of many. We live in a dark world today.

The psalmist exclaims to God, 'The unfolding of your words gives light …' (Psa. 119:130). Light in the darkness. As we unfold God's Word during this Advent season, may it illumine our minds and our hearts. In the same psalm we read, 'Your word is a lamp to my feet and a light for my path' (v.105). Let us walk in that light. Let it guide our steps. The apostle John tells us of light shining in the darkness when 'The Word became flesh' (John 1:14). This is what we celebrate at Christmastime. Let us live in that light. And let us pray for our world, that the light of the gospel will shine in the darkness and that many more people will turn to the One who is the Light of the world.

How to use *The Light of the World*

This book will take you through the month of December a
day at a time. Each day's short Bible reading is reproduced
in full and is followed by a brief meditation or comment as
well as ideas for applying the Bible text. As you read the
material each day, take the time to think it through in order
to enter more fully and more deeply into God's purposes.
We begin with the account of the creation of the world and
move on through the Old Testament – looking particularly
at the book of Job, some of the prophets and the psalms –
into the Gospels and the announcement of Jesus' birth. We
see what Jesus Himself teaches about light. Then, following
His death and resurrection and ascension, the writers of
the New Testament letters encourage us to look forward to
the time when Jesus will come again. Finally, some of the
verses in the book of Revelation help us to focus on the
consummation of God's will for His world. We are told that
'There will be no more night' (Rev. 22:5).

Group use
As you meditate progressively on the theme of darkness
and light as it occurs throughout the Scriptures, you may
wish to share your thoughts with others. For that reason
there are some suggestions for reflection and discussion
following each day's meditation. The material for each day
concludes with either a short prayer or a suggestion as to
how you might pray either on your own or with others.

From Light to Darkness

In the account of the creation, we read: 'Now the earth was formless and empty, darkness was over the surface of the deep ...' (Gen. 1:2). 'Darkness' often conveys the idea of gloom, depression, desolation, isolation, evil or chaos. God brings order out of chaos. The text in Genesis continues:

> And God said, 'Let there be light,' and there was light. God saw that the light was good, and he separated the light from the darkness. God called the light 'day', and the darkness he called 'night' ...
>
> And God said, 'Let there be lights in the expanse of the sky to separate the day from the night, and let them serve as signs to mark seasons and days and years, and let them be lights in the expanse of the sky to give light on the earth.' And it was so. God made two great lights – the greater light to govern the day and the lesser light to govern the night. He also made the stars. God set them in the expanse of the sky to give light on the earth, to govern the day and the night, and to separate light from darkness.
>
> Genesis 1:3–5,14–18

To express their suffering, people have often picked up on the title of a sixteenth-century poem written by St John of the Cross: 'Dark night of the soul'. God brings comfort and hope to people whose lives are marked by disorder of one kind or another. As David Atkinson says in his commentary on Genesis, 'He hovers over your darkness and says, "Let there be light".'[1]

Light was gone

Light for your path

> I looked at the earth,
>   and it was formless and empty;
> and at the heavens,
>   and their light was gone.
> I looked at the mountains
>   and they were quaking;
>   all the hills were swaying.
> I looked, and there were no people;
>   every bird in the sky had flown away.
> I looked, and the fruitful land was a desert;
>   all its towns lay in ruins
>   before the LORD, before his fierce anger.
>
> This is what the LORD says:
>
> 'The whole land will be ruined ...
> the earth will mourn
>   and the heavens above grow dark ...'

Jeremiah 4:23–28

I'm sure we've all been discouraged at times, when working through a difficult situation, to realise that when we hoped we were making progress we were in fact 'back to square one'! That is basically what Jeremiah says in our passage today. He paints a prophetic picture of bleakness and desolation. Disaster has struck. Some of the words Jeremiah uses to describe this catastrophe are identical to the words in Genesis 1:1: '... the earth was formless and empty ...' Darkness once again covered the earth. There was no more light. The life-giving light that God had set in the sky was no more. Why? God's people had been unfaithful to Him. They had turned to pagan deities. He was grieved and angry with them.

Four times in these verses Jeremiah says, 'I looked'. He could not take his eyes off these different aspects of a ruined land. He saw the deserted wasteland with its quaking mountains and swaying hills. The landscape was devoid of people. There was not a bird to be seen. The 'towns lay in ruins' (v.26). Does this description conjure up scenes of desolation seen on your TV screens in recent years?

However, amidst the darkness and destruction there is a glimmer of light. When the Lord says that 'The whole land will be ruined', He adds, 'though I will not destroy it completely' (v.27). This note of hope emerges repeatedly throughout the Old Testament and finds fulfilment in the coming of the Messiah.

Shedding light

At some period in life we all go through dark times. Right now you may be coping with some form of suffering – illness, bereavement, job loss, financial difficulties, family problems ... You probably know other people who are facing hard times too. Does it help you to know that you are not alone in your anguish? Can you say with the same assurance as the prophet Micah, 'Though I sit in darkness, the LORD will be my light' (Micah 7:8)?

There are times too when we may have to face the consequences of our sin. We might be tempted – like God's people at the time Jeremiah was writing – to turn away from God to idols. Anyone or anything that takes the place of God in our lives could be deemed an 'idol'. But let us always remember that

There's a way back to God from the dark paths of sin;
There's a door that is open and you may go in:
At Calvary's cross is where you begin,
When you come as a sinner to Jesus.

E.H. Swinstead[2]

Let your light shine

1. Jeremiah says he 'looked at the earth'. What do you see when

you look at the earth at this time of the year? I walked out in freezing temperatures and brilliant sunshine. The snowy mountains in the distance are lit up by the sun's rays. Late roses are bathed in golden light. The waves on Lake Geneva, just over the border from where I live, freeze as they hit the trees along the lakeside, creating marvellous icy designs. What can we learn about God as we look at His world?

2. Have you ever literally been plunged into darkness? How did you feel?
3. What recent scenes of desolation does Jeremiah's description remind you of? The earthquake in China in 2008, or in Italy in 2009? The tsunami in 2004? Results of terrorist attacks or military bombardments?

Light to live by

Pray for survivors of the catastrophes mentioned above, many of whom have been bereaved, injured, maimed and psychologically disturbed. Pray that they might get the help they need and that they might turn to Jesus, the Light of the world.

2 Dec

Darkness and deep shadow

Light for your path

'May the day of my birth perish,
  and the night it was said, 'A boy is born!'
That day – may it turn to darkness;
  may God above not care about it;
  may no light shine upon it.
May darkness and deep shadow claim it once more;
  may a cloud settle over it;
  may blackness overwhelm its light.
That night – may thick darkness seize it ...
May its morning stars become dark;
  may it wait for daylight in vain
  and not see the first rays of dawn ...'

Job 3:3–6,9

The theme of darkness and light occurs many times in the book of Job. Some of the verses we shall look at this week will reveal to us that when Job was in the depths of despair, he had the impression that the light had gone from his life and that he was plunged into utter darkness.

We know, from the first chapter of the book of Job, that he 'was blameless and upright; he feared God and shunned evil ... He was the greatest man among all the people of the East' (Job 1:1,3). Satan suggested to God that Job only remained faithful to Him because of all the many blessings that God had poured out upon him. He wanted to test Job to see if he would end up cursing God. God told Satan to go ahead. So, in a short space of time, Job lost his livestock and his children. Then Satan 'afflicted Job with painful sores from the soles of his feet to the top of his head' (Job 2:7). We read that 'In all this, Job did not sin by charging God with wrongdoing' (Job 1:22). However, he did begin to wish he had never been born. He 'cursed the day of his birth' (Job 3:1), using vivid pictures of darkness and light to convey his pain, anguish and grief.

he lost his work, his family (+ legacy) and his health

Shedding light

Without going so far as to curse the day they were born, many people can look back to experiences in their childhood that have impacted negatively upon them and have caused ongoing suffering.

Violence in the home during his childhood had a long-term effect on Gram Seed[3] and contributed to his life of crime, alcoholism and drug addiction. Homeless and hopeless, unloved and not far from death, Gram was told that Jesus loved him. Sceptical at first, he later responded to God's offer of salvation in Jesus. He stepped out of darkness into God's 'wonderful light' (1 Pet. 2:9). Now he reaches out to others in need, so that they too may meet the One who is the Light of the world.

Let your light shine

1. What kind of childhood did you have? Look back over your life. Reflect on the good times and the bad.
2. What does it mean to you to know that God has 'called you out of darkness into his wonderful light' (1 Pet. 2:9)? *life-changing*
3. How far can you identify with Job in his suffering?
   More than I ever thought possible.

4. We know – thanks to the explanation given in the first two
chapters of the book of Job – that Job's trials were deliberately
inflicted upon him by Satan. Satan is still active today. Reflect on
ways in which the devil might try to cause you to fall. The Bible
tells us to 'Resist the devil, and he will flee from [us]' (James 4:7).
How can we best resist him?

Light to live by
Thank the Lord for the good times you have experienced. Talk
to Him about the bad times. Ask Him to let His light shine in any
dark corners of your life. Bring to Him your fears, your doubts, any
negative feelings or unresolved problems. Draw close to Him. Praise
Him because He has 'called you out of darkness into his wonderful
light' (1 Pet. 2:9).

3 Dec

Walking through darkness

Light for your path

'How I long for the months gone by,
  for the days when God watched over me,
when his lamp shone upon my head
  and by his light I walked through darkness!'

Job 29:2–3

In the midst of his suffering, Job spends quite some time reminiscing.
He remembers the good old days when his children were alive and
God was with him, when he was respected by young and old alike
(see Job 29:1–17). 'Job's first memories are of a rich and harmonious
relationship with his God ... "Lamp" and "light" are symbols of God's
blessing and protection.'[4] He longs for those happy times again, when
the light of God's presence illuminated his path and led him through
the darkness. But for the time being, Job's hopes will not be realised.
On the contrary, he continues, 'When I hoped for good, evil came;
when I looked for light, then came darkness' (Job 30:26). What a

terrifying, destabilising experience! 'Everything that Job once believed was turned upside down; the result is emotional and spiritual turmoil.'[5]

Shedding light

Job had had a long, happy, enriching relationship with God. Then suddenly all went haywire. We know why (see Job 1–2). But Job was kept in ignorance. Things got so bad that all he wanted to do was die. He told his friends that he was going to 'the place of no return, to the land of gloom and deep shadow, to the land of deepest night, of deep shadow and disorder, where even the light is like darkness' (Job 10:21–22). What a description! Even mature Christians can have doubts and can fall into despair. Circumstances of our lives can very easily rock the boat. We pray, but God does not seem to answer. We cry out to Him, but He does not seem to hear. All seems dark. What do we do then? Isaiah gives us the solution. He says, 'Let him who walks in the dark, who has no light, trust in the name of the LORD and rely on his God' (Isa. 50:10). In spite of everything, we must trust God; we must rely on Him, count on Him. In spite of appearances and circumstances, He is completely worthy of our trust. 'The LORD is my light and my salvation,' exclaimed the psalmist (Psa. 27:1). Whatever happens, let us always hold on to Him. Once again, our thoughts turn to the psalmist's description of God's Word that we have already mentioned in the introduction to this book: 'Your word is a lamp to my feet and a light for my path' (Psa. 119:105). Let us continue to read God's Word, to study God's Word. God's Word shines through the darkness, showing us which way to go. It will lead us to the One whose birth we soon will celebrate, the Son of God who said, 'I am the light of the world. Whoever follows me will never walk in darkness, but will have the light of life' (John 8:12).

Let your light shine

1. How do you feel when God seems absent, when He doesn't seem to hear your cries?
2. How do you react when you feel you are walking in the dark? What can you do practically?
3. Can you echo the psalmist's words, 'The LORD is my light and my salvation' (Psa. 27:1)? What do they mean to you?
4. What part does God's Word play in your life?

Light to live by

Lord, help me to trust You at all times. I want to be able to trust You even when all seems dark, when You seem far away and You don't seem to hear my cries or answer my prayers. I know, Lord, that You have promised never to leave me. I know that You want the best for me. I know that You love me. Thank You for loving me enough to send the Saviour into the world. Thank You for Jesus, the Light of the world, who loved me enough to die for me.

4 Dec

Driven from light into darkness

Light for your path

'The lamp of the wicked is snuffed out;
  the flame of his fire stops burning.
The light in his tent becomes dark;
  the lamp beside him goes out …
He is driven from light into darkness
  and is banished from the world.'

Job 18:5–6,18

Job's friends no doubt meant well, but they were totally insensitive to his feelings. They tended to think he had brought all his troubles upon himself. Today's verses express their evaluation of Job's situation. Using the analogy of light turning to darkness, Job's friend Bildad implies that Job is evil and that he cannot possibly know God (see also v.21). Bildad is far too cut and dried and black and white in his comments. He draws wrong conclusions. He professes to know and understand God. How pretentious! During this Advent season, we are preparing to celebrate the time when God, in His mercy, revealed Himself to human beings in the Person of His Son. We can 'know' God through Jesus, but I don't think any of us would profess to understand Him. Our minds cannot grasp Him. He is infinite. As King Solomon said, '… the heavens, even the highest heavens, cannot contain him …' (2 Chron. 2:6). He is completely 'other'. He is almighty, sovereign and transcendent. We can only bow down before Him and worship.

Shedding light

I have a Finnish friend who suffers from 'winter depressions'. Dark days can take the joy out of life. She is conscious of 'suffering and grief' even in the small Swiss town where she lives: 'severe illness, death, divorce, loneliness, problems with the younger generation ...' She continues, 'And it is precisely in this darkness that the eternal God comes and offers us His gift – forgiveness, peace and hope in Jesus! Are we so busy with wrapping paper and decorations that we no longer even want to remember why we actually celebrate Christmas? Do His light and His love still reach our hearts in this other gloomy valley?'[6]

As we look ahead to Christmas, we rejoice at the coming of the Saviour into the world. How wonderful to be able to enter into a relationship with God through Jesus! Because of Jesus, we can call God our 'Father' and enjoy intimacy with Him. We can talk to God and listen to Him. We can spend time in His presence. 'Be still, and know that I am God,' He says (Psa. 46:10). We can learn about God through His Word. But let us never think that we can understand Him completely. And if ever we are called upon to reach out to people in distress, let us not fall into the trap of Job's friends. It is only too easy to construct some form of system and expect everything to fall into place and conform to our way of thinking. As we have seen from the book of Job, things are not always what they seem. We need to be sensitive and loving and caring as we relate to those who hurt. Let us draw alongside them and seek to empathise with them in their suffering.

Let your light shine

1. How do you put into practice the exhortation, 'Be still, and know that I am God'?
2. How could you best befriend someone who, like Job, has lost what he or she cherished most?
3. Jesus said to His disciples, 'You are the light of the world' (Matt. 5:14). In what sense do you think that Christians today are (or should be) 'the light of the world'?

Light to live by
'Even though I walk through the valley of the shadow of death, I will fear no evil, for you are with me; your rod and your staff, they comfort me' (Psa. 23:4). Thank You, Lord, for Your comfort. Thank You too for coming to earth as a helpless baby and for identifying with sinful humanity. Thank You for dying so that I might live.

Spend time worshipping God. Then pray for those you know who are going through deep suffering. Pray for sensitivity and wisdom and understanding and discernment and love as you have the opportunity of reaching out to them.

5 Dec

The place of light and darkness

Light for your path

... the LORD answered Job out of the storm. He said:

'Who is this that darkens my counsel
  with words without knowledge? ...
Where were you when I laid the earth's foundation?
  Tell me, if you understand.
Who marked off its dimensions? Surely you know!
  Who stretched a measuring line across it?
On what were its footings set,
  or who laid its cornerstone –
while the morning stars sang together
  and all the angels shouted for joy? ...
What is the way to the abode of light?
And where does darkness reside?'

Job 38:1,4–7,19

In chapter 38 of the book of Job, God Himself speaks. Job's friends have had their say. Now God answers Job. He speaks 'out of the storm' (v.1) of Job's confusion and darkness, his anguish and loss, his suffering and pain. It is interesting to note that the way

God 'answers' Job is in fact by asking questions! Responding to questions helps us to think through an issue and come to our own conclusions. Of course, there are such things as rhetorical questions, questions that do not need an answer. And when God asks Job, 'Where were you when I laid the earth's foundation?' (v.4) and 'Who marked off its dimensions?' (v.5), as well as His questions about light and darkness, He is not really expecting Job to answer. Rather, He is emphasising His own sovereignty and omnipotence. As the apostle Paul says, '... since the creation of the world God's invisible qualities – his eternal power and divine nature – have been clearly seen ...' (Rom. 1:20). In today's passage, God is referring back to creation, but doesn't verse 7 ('all the angels shouted for joy') remind you of the night when Jesus was born? Luke tells us that, 'An angel of the Lord appeared to them [some shepherds], and the glory of the Lord shone around them ... the angel said to them, "... I bring you good news of great joy that will be for all the people. Today in the town of David a Saviour has been born to you; he is Christ the Lord ... Suddenly a great company of the heavenly host appeared with the angel, praising God ...' (Luke 2:9–11,13).

Shedding light

Throughout his sufferings – even though he could not understand the reason for them – Job remained faithful to God. Similarly, we might not understand why we are going through storms, and why trials come upon us. We may be tempted to 'Curse God and die!' (Job 2:9), which is what Job's wife urged him to do. But just as God revealed Himself to Job, so He can teach us much about Himself in our times of darkness. And He can turn our darkness into light. 'You are my lamp, O LORD,' said David. He continues, '... the LORD turns my darkness into light' (2 Sam. 22:29). In fact, God had promised David that he would 'always have a lamp' (1 Kings 11:36; 2 Kings 8:19). As Fergus Macdonald points out, this lamp 'would in the person of David's greatest Son become the Light of the world.'[7]

Let your light shine

1. What are God's 'invisible qualities'? How do you perceive them? (See Romans 1:20.)

2. What have you learned about God during times of 'darkness'?
3. What experiences have you been through that would enable you
   to say, 'The LORD turns my darkness into light' (2 Sam. 22:29)?

Light to live by

> O LORD, you have searched me and you know me.
> You know when I sit and when I rise;
>   you perceive my thoughts from afar.
> You discern my going out and my lying down;
>   you are familiar with all my ways.
> Before a word is on my tongue
>   you know it completely, O LORD …
> Where can I go from your Spirit?
>   Where can I flee from your presence? …
> If I say, 'Surely the darkness will hide me
>   and the light become night around me,'
> even the darkness will not be dark to you;
>   the night will shine like the day,
>   for darkness is as light to you …
>
> Psalm 139:1–4,7,11–12

6 Dec

Darkness, not light

Light for your path

> Woe to you who long
>   for the day of the LORD!
> Why do you long for the day of the LORD?
>   That day will be darkness, not light.
> It will be as though a man fled from a lion
>   only to meet a bear,
> as though he entered his house
>   and rested his hand on the wall
>   only to have a snake bite him.

> Will not the day of the LORD be darkness, not light –
> pitch-dark, without a ray of brightness?
>
> Amos 5:18–20

Have you ever rested your hand on the wall in your own home
only to have a snake bite you? Or maybe you have put your feet
into your slippers on awaking one morning only to find a scorpion
in there! In some countries this could easily happen. I spent my
childhood in Africa and have memories of unwelcome visitors
invading our home! One's home would normally be thought of as
being comfortable and secure, but sometimes there are surprises
– bad surprises. Amos has already made clear to God's people, in
the preceding verses, why 'the day of the LORD' will actually 'be
darkness, not light' for them. It is because of their sin (see Amos
5:11–12). These outwardly religious people were looking forward
to the time when the Lord would come, but they did not see that they
needed to repent. 'Seek me and live,' says God to His people (v.4).
'Seek good, not evil, that you may live,' says the prophet (v.14).
They were like some of the religious leaders in the time of Jesus,
who were hypocritical and who exploited the poor. 'What good
is it for a man to gain the whole world, yet forfeit his soul?' asked
Jesus (Mark 8:36). Judgment was inevitable. We all deserve to be
condemned. 'There is no-one righteous, not even one,' wrote Paul
(Rom. 3:10). How wonderful then, that when the Lord did come, He
came not to judge us but to save us. He Himself paid the price. He
died in our place. He submitted to the darkness of Calvary so that
we might have the light of life.

Shedding light

The people Amos was addressing were looking forward to 'the day
of the Lord', the time when He would come in Person. But in fact,
in spite of their religiosity, their inconsistent behaviour caused them
rather to distance themselves from the Lord. This still happens today.
'People of profession without reality, of religion without the evidence
of spiritual and moral transformation are moving in precisely the
wrong direction, away from God.'[8] How can such people – who may
be churchgoers without ever really having understood the message
of salvation in Jesus – be drawn to Him? Maybe this Advent time

is an opportunity for us to try to get across the real message of the gospel, so that the light of God's Word will shine into the dark corners of people's minds and cause them to turn to the One who is the Light of the world.

Let your light shine
1. How and when did you first understand the gospel and move from darkness to light?
2. How can you best reach out to people who seem to be religious, but who have never entered into a relationship with Jesus? How could you share the message of the gospel with them?
3. What do you understand by 'the day of the Lord'? Do you long for 'the day of the Lord'? Why?

Light to live by
Thank the Lord for His wonderful gift of salvation in Jesus. Thank Him for people He used to draw you to Himself. Pray for people you know who have not yet understood their need of Him. Pray that the light of the gospel will shine into their hearts, dispelling the darkness. Pray that they might turn to Him in repentance and faith.

7 Dec

The light of life

Light for your path

> In God, whose word I praise,
>   in the LORD, whose word I praise –
> in God I trust; I will not be afraid.
>   What can man do to me?
>
> I am under vows to you, O God;
> I will present my thank-offerings to you.
> For you have delivered me from death
>   and my feet from stumbling,

that I may walk before God
in the light of life.

Psalm 56:10–13

The heading in my Bible says that this is a psalm of David. It would
seem that it refers to the time 'When the Philistines had seized
him in Gath'. David talks about being pursued and attacked. He
was obviously afraid, but determined to trust in God. In the verses
quoted above, it would seem that the Lord has delivered him. His
trust in God dispels his fear. 'In God I trust; I will not be afraid,'
he says. David's response reminds me of the words of the apostle
Paul: 'If God is for us, who can be against us?' (Rom. 8:31). What
a transformation in David's situation: he left the darkness of his
suffering for 'the light of life'. It seems that he had made a vow to
God to follow Him and obey Him if he were delivered from the
enemy. He is concerned to keep his vows. The words concluding
our passage today are identical to those found in John's Gospel
chapter 8 and verse 12. Jesus is speaking and He says: 'I am the light
of the world. Whoever follows me will never walk in darkness, but
will have the light of life.'

Shedding light
If we, like David, choose to 'walk before God in the light of life',
we will walk in fellowship with Him. We will follow Him and obey
Him. C.H. Spurgeon thought that 'the light of life' could also refer
to those living in the light, which means we would also be walking
in fellowship with other believers. How precious it is to meet with
other Christians, to have the opportunity of worshipping together,
praying together, studying God's Word together and growing together
in the faith. Together we can reach out to those around us who are
still in darkness. We can invite them to follow Jesus and have 'the
light of life'.

Walk in the light, so shalt thou know
That fellowship of love
His Spirit only can bestow,
Who reigns in light above.

Walk in the light, and thou shalt find
Thy heart made truly His,
Who dwells in cloudless light enshrined,
In Whom no darkness is.

Walk in the light – and sin abhorred
Shall not defile again;
The blood of Jesus Christ the Lord
Shall cleanse from every stain.

Walk in the light, and e'en the tomb
No fearful shade shall wear;
Glory shall chase away its gloom,
For Christ hath conquered there.

Walk in the light, and thou shalt own
Thy darkness passed away,
Because that light hath on thee shone,
In which is perfect day.

Walk in the light – thy path shall be
Peaceful, serene, and bright;
For God, by grace, shall dwell in thee,
And God Himself is Light.

Bernard Barton (1784–1849)

Let your light shine
1. If you have time, read the whole of Psalm 56. Identify with David in his fear of the Philistines and in his cries for help to God. Then notice the change in Him as he begins to trust God and praise Him for his deliverance.
2. What does it mean to you to have 'the light of life'?
3. How important is it to you to be 'together' with other Christians?

Light to live by

Thank You, Lord, for Your protection, for Your deliverance and for Your salvation. Like David, I want to walk before You in the light of life. Thank You for my brothers and sisters in Christ. May we be an encouragement to one another.

1. David Atkinson, *The Message of Genesis 1–11* (Leicester: IVP, 1990) p.25.
2. E.H. Swinstead (d.1976), 'There's a Way Back to God'. All reasonable effort was made to find the copyright holder of this hymn.
3. Gram Seed, *One Step Beyond* (Farnham: CWR, 2008).
4. Norman C. Habel, *The Book of Job* (Philadelphia: The Westminster Press, 1985) p.409.
5. Ibid., p.422.
6. Riitta Steiner, quoted with permission.
7. Fergus Macdonald, *Encounter with God*, January–March 2009 (Milton Keynes: Scripture Union) p.31.
8. J.A. Motyer in D.A. Carson, R.T. France, J.A. Motyer & G.J. Wenham, *New Bible Commentary, 21st century edition* (Leicester: IVP, 1994) p.802.

Light Dawns

I hope the first week of readings was not too depressing! I wanted us to see – through Job's experiences and from the experiences of others, and sometimes because of our own choices and priorities – how dark life can be. By contrast, we were able to see how brightly light shines in the darkness. I recently had a time of fellowship with a friend who is going through some very trying circumstances. She made the point as she shared and we prayed together, that one small candle is sufficient to light up a dark place.

Last week we started off with the story of the creation of the world. There is a strong connection between the beginning of Genesis and the beginning of John's Gospel. The first three words of the book of Genesis are identical to those of John's Gospel: 'In the beginning ...' 'In the beginning God created the heavens and the earth' (Gen. 1:1), and 'In the beginning was the Word ...' (John 1:1). Then in the Genesis account we read that 'God said, "Let there be light," ...' (Gen. 1:3). In John's Gospel, we read that 'the Word ... was with God in the beginning ... In him was life, and that life was the light of men. The light shines in the darkness, but the darkness has not understood it' (John 1:1–2,4–5). Other versions read: '... the darkness did not overcome it' or '... the darkness couldn't put it out.' The light continues to shine. The darkness has never been able to put it out. We know that John was referring to Jesus, 'the light of the world'. He is the true light and He continues to shine. No amount of darkness could ever extinguish His light.

Darkness for light and light for darkness

Light for your path

Woe to those who call evil good
  and good evil,
who put darkness for light
  and light for darkness,
who put bitter for sweet
  and sweet for bitter ...
And if one looks at the land,
  he will see darkness and distress;
  even the light will be darkened by the clouds.

Isaiah 5:20,30

In these verses, Isaiah could easily be describing our twenty-first-century world. Basically he is saying that sin has become an accepted way of life. People consider themselves to be autonomous. They can, therefore, do what they like. They can indulge themselves to the limit. Unfortunately, during the Advent season that is often what happens. God is not indifferent to these distortions. Isaiah tells us that 'the LORD's anger burns' (v.25). Judgment will fall. The light disappears as the dark clouds gather.

We could say that the people Isaiah was referring to were 'slaves to sin'. The apostle Paul used that very expression when he wrote to the Christians in Rome: 'For we know that our old self was crucified with him [Christ] so that the body of sin might be done away with, that we should no longer be slaves to sin ...' (Rom. 6:6). Without Jesus, we are all 'slaves to sin.' But, as Paul exhorts the Roman believers, we too can 'count ... [ourselves] dead to sin but alive to God in Christ Jesus' (Rom. 6:11). In Jesus we pass from death to life, from darkness to light.

Shedding light

It is not easy to discuss with people in our postmodern society, because what might be true for one person could very well not be true for another. What I might qualify as wrong is (they would say) only my opinion. What is wrong for me might be right for someone else. There are no absolutes. As long as people continue to see themselves as unaccountable to anyone else, and particularly as unaccountable to God, they will continue to do whatever they like. We only have to glance at our newspapers or watch TV to see selfishness and different forms of immorality across the whole spectrum of life. It is 'normal'. Some people think they can get away with anything. There is no thought of judgment in their minds. We know from what the apostle Peter wrote that 'The Lord ... is patient ... not wanting anyone to perish, but everyone to come to repentance' (2 Pet. 3:9). But Peter makes it clear that judgment – sooner or later – will fall. It is inevitable. We have a choice: life or death; light or darkness. Moses put before the Israelites this same choice: '... I have set before you life and death, blessings and curses. Now choose life, so that you ... may live ...' (Deut. 30:19).

Let your light shine

1. How do you feel you relate to people in our postmodern society?
2. How can we get across to people the message of salvation and the need to repent?
3. How can we make them understand the wonder of the 'light of life' (John 8:12) that Jesus promises to those who follow Him?

Light to live by

Lord, keep us from shrugging our shoulders and seeing as 'normal' the sin that abounds in the world. Help us to remember that 'where sin abounded, grace did much more abound' (Rom. 5:20, AV). May we rejoice in our salvation as we try to spread the light of the gospel around us.

9 Dec

No more gloom

Light for your path

> Some sat in darkness and the deepest gloom ...
> Then they cried to the LORD in their trouble,
>   and he saved them from their distress.
> He brought them out of darkness and the deepest gloom ...
>
> Psalm 107:10,13–14

> ... they will look towards the earth and see only distress and darkness and fearful gloom, and they will be thrust into utter darkness.
> Nevertheless, there will be no more gloom for those who were in distress ...

> The people walking in darkness
>   have seen a great light;
> on those living in the land of the shadow of death
>   a light has dawned ...
> For to us a child is born,
>   to us a son is given,
>   and the government will be on his shoulders.
>
> Isaiah 8:22–9:2,6

The verses quoted from Psalm 107 refer to prisoners. They were in chains because 'they had rebelled against the words of God and despised the counsel of the Most High' (v.11). The final verse of Isaiah chapter 8 gives a picture of captives too. We are told that these people had rejected God and refused His law. These two examples – taken from two different books of the Old Testament – are very similar. The language is graphic: distress, darkness, deepest gloom. Then in both cases there is a complete transformation. What happened to bring the transformation about? In Psalm 107 we read that the prisoners 'cried to the LORD in their trouble, and he saved them from their distress' (v.13). Interestingly, the verses from Isaiah, although referring to a future event, are written in the past tense. This gives us the certainty and assurance that what Isaiah predicts will definitely happen. For 'the people walking in darkness ...' this prophecy must have truly been words of hope. As Alec Motyer says in his commentary on Isaiah, '... those walking in the darkness can see the light ahead and are sustained by hope.'[1] Matthew tells us that Jesus fulfilled Isaiah's prophecy (see Matt. 4:13–16).

Shedding light

Can you see the light ahead during this period of Advent? Maybe you feel imprisoned by some experience you are going through, or by a relationship, or by a sin you have committed, or by some form of rebellion, or for some other reason. Can you see the light ahead? You are in distress, in darkness, in deepest gloom. Can you see the light ahead? As I write this, I have learned that friends of mine have suffered several bereavements in a very short space of time. This has plunged them into distress and darkness and deepest gloom. I wonder if they can see the light ahead? I pray that they will. Whatever darkness we might be going through right now, there is light ahead. Isaiah talks too of rejoicing. He gives the reason for the joy: 'For to us a child is born, to us a son is given, and the government will be on his shoulders. And he will be called Wonderful Counsellor, Mighty God, Everlasting Father, Prince of Peace' (9:6). Our Christmas newsletter last year began with these words: 'In a world full of uncertainties and tensions, in an age of ever increasing violence and lawlessness and of deep spiritual darkness, where economic crises and personal trials disturb and distress us, *I'm glad the government is on His shoulders.*'

Let your light shine

1. When going through times of distress and darkness, what does it mean to you to know that there is light ahead?
2. How do you feel about Advent? Is it a time of hope, a time of preparation, a time of waiting, a time of frustration, a time of confusion, a time of joy, a time of pain ...?
3. Read Psalm 107:10–16. In what way could you follow the example of those prisoners?

Light to live by

Thank You, Lord, that the prophecy of Isaiah has been fulfilled. Thank You for dispelling the darkness. Thank You that the 'great light' shone – and continues to shine – in a dark world. Thank You, Almighty God, for the Child that was born, for the Son that was given.

10 Dec

Darkness turned to light

Light for your path

'I will lead the blind by ways they have not known,
   along unfamiliar paths I will guide them;
I will turn the darkness into light before them
   and make the rough places smooth.'

Isaiah 42:16

For nearly three days heavy clouds and falling snow obscured the view from our living room window. Then suddenly a bright beam of light began to shine between the dark clouds. This gradually spread as the clouds dispersed, and the whole sky became dazzling, too bright for me to look at. At the same time everything in the room was illuminated. What a transformation! I lifted up my face to the light and thanked God that He can transform situations in the same way, by shining His light into the darkness, indeed by turning darkness into light.

In the above quote from Isaiah, God graciously promises to lead His people out of exile. Even though they are like blind people crossing unknown territory, He will guide them. He will show them the way. Indeed, we know that He *is* the way. He 'will turn the darkness into light before them and make the rough places smooth'. They will be able to trust Him completely as He transforms their situation. He is all-powerful. No obstacle is too difficult for Him to negotiate.

Shedding light

How wonderful to know that God will do the same for His children today. He has promised never to leave us, so we know that we can always count on Him. We can trust Him completely. He will guide us and direct us. He can transform any situation in which we might find ourselves. He can use our difficult experiences to transform *us* and make us more like Jesus. You may be far from home and feel as if you are 'in exile'. You may be walking over 'rough places' and along 'unfamiliar paths'. Remember the verse we have already quoted more than once: 'Your word is a lamp to my feet and a light for my path' (Psa. 119:105). Your 'unfamiliar paths' can be lit up by God's Word. They can be illuminated by God's presence. The darkest hour is before dawn. Ask God to turn your darkness into light and to make your rough places smooth. Put your hand in His and let Him lead you. As David said, 'He guides me in paths of righteousness for his name's sake' (Psa. 23:3).

> Light has dawned that ever shall blaze,
> Darkness flees away;
> Christ the light has shone in our hearts,
> Turning night to day.
>
> Graham Kendrick © 1988 Make Way Music.
> www.grahamkendrick.co.uk[2]

Let your light shine

1. What experience in your life could be compared to being in exile? How do you feel in that particular situation?
2. What 'unfamiliar paths' and 'rough places' are you negotiating at present?
3. What difference does it make to you to bring God into the difficult areas of your life?

Light to live by

Thank You, Lord, for the wonderful promises in Your Word. Thank You that You are all-powerful and You can transform situations. You can turn darkness into light and make the rough places smooth. Lord, please do that for me. Lead me and guide me, Lord, I pray.

Pray for anyone you know who may feel 'in exile'. Ask the Lord to transform their situation, to turn their darkness into light and make the rough places smooth.

11 Dec

Shining like stars

Light for your path

> 'You are the light of the world. A city on a hill cannot be hidden. Neither do people light a lamp and put it under a bowl. Instead they put it on its stand, and it gives light to everyone in the house. In the same way, let your light shine before men, that they may see your good deeds and praise your Father in heaven.'
>
> Matthew 5:14–16

In 2008, to celebrate the fortieth anniversary of the death of Martin Luther King, our church organised four days and evenings of special events. We had an exhibition reflecting his life and ministry. We had special meetings, a film and a gospel choir. We tried to reach out to the surrounding area with a message of light and hope and freedom in Christ. One phrase of Martin Luther King that stuck with me is: 'Darkness cannot dispel darkness; only light can.' I think Matthew says something similar in the above verses.

Jesus considers His followers to be 'the light of the world', just as He is Himself. 'Until He has illuminated us, we can never shine with His reflected light.'[3] Light is visible. We should be as noticeable as 'a city on a hill'. Other people should benefit from our light, just as the light that is on a stand 'gives light to everyone in the house'. The apostle Paul says we should 'shine like stars in the universe' (Phil. 2:15). I have shared elsewhere[4] that I once had the opportunity of observing the stars with an astronomer in Australia's Red Centre. Because we were in the desert, far away from the lights of any town, the stars shone even more brightly in the dark sky. As Jesus says, there is no point in lighting a lamp if we then hide it away under a bowl. We are to live in such a way that people will notice our 'good deeds'. This should result, not in their complimenting us, but in praising God who is the source of our light.

Shedding light

Jesus indicates that His followers should be fully involved in society. If we are to be 'the light of the world', then we need to be 'in' the world even though we are not 'of' it (see John 17:11,14). Jesus said to His disciples, 'you do not belong to the world' (John 15:19). He sent them into the world as a light, just as He Himself came into the world as a light (see John 12:46).

Depending on your gifts and resources you might be active in local politics, or you could help in a relief organisation or in a local school. A friend of ours has a correspondence with a prisoner on death row in Texas. You might want to get to know your neighbours better and be a light in your neighbourhood. When I retired I joined a gym class. Besides its physical benefits, this activity has also been a means of getting to know people. At the same time I started a monthly book club in our home to which I invited a few friends and acquaintances, some Christian, some not. The idea was to read and discuss secular literature. In so doing, it is often possible to express a biblical point of view. Now, a few years later, several people from the gym class also attend my book club and of those, some have also attended events at our church. During Advent the members of the club are invited to share a Christmas story. This is an opportunity to convey to them the real meaning of Christmas.

Let your light shine

1. Think of ways to let your light shine in the world, using your gifts and any opportunities that might come your way.
2. How can your 'good deeds' cause people to praise God?
3. In what ways might you be tempted to put your lamp 'under a bowl'?

Light to live by

Lord, it's not always easy to be light in this world. I need You with me. Thank You that You have promised never to leave me. I need wisdom and discernment, Lord, in knowing what to do and what to say. Show me how I can be more involved in my local community.

Help me to get across the real message of Christmas, that Jesus came into the world to save sinners.

12 Dec

Walking in the dark

Light for your path

> Who among you fears the LORD
>   and obeys the word of his servant?
> Let him who walks in the dark,
>   who has no light,
> trust in the name of the LORD
>   and rely on his God.
> But now, all of you who light fires
>   and provide yourselves with flaming torches,
> go, walk in the light of your fires
>   and of the torches you have set ablaze.
>
> Isaiah 50:10–11

These verses from the prophet Isaiah are part of what is generally known as the third 'Servant Song', the 'Servant' being a prophetic term for Christ. The prophet is telling those who fear the Lord and obey Him to trust Him completely, to rely on Him, even though the way ahead might be very dark. (When the Bible talks about fearing God, it does not mean that we are afraid of Him, but that we are in awe of Him and we reverence Him.) In fact it is pitch dark with not even a flicker or a glimmer of light. Have you ever found yourself in such darkness literally? Apart from feeling panic-stricken, one would also be completely disorientated. One would be stumbling about, not knowing which way to turn. Of course, we can have those kinds of feelings too when we are going through dark times. We cannot see the way ahead. We may be paralysed by fear or by grief. Anyone going through such utter darkness is exhorted to 'trust in the name of the LORD and rely on his God'. I'm so glad Isaiah said '*his* God' (my italics), because the possessive adjective 'his' denotes a relationship.

'God' might seem far off, but 'his' God (or 'my' God) brings Him very close. I know that the One I am trusting and relying on is completely worthy of my trust. He loves me and wants the best for me. However, those who have prepared fires of destruction destined for the 'Servant' will face those fires of judgment themselves.

Shedding light

'Flaming torches' can be pretty dramatic! Every year in mid-December, at nightfall, a procession of men on horseback wearing period costume and carrying flaming torches winds through the streets of the Old Town of Geneva, commemorating an event known as the 'Escalade' that took place on 12 December 1602, when neighbouring French Catholics tried to scale the walls and take over this protestant city. One can easily get caught up in the drama as those flaming torches defiantly penetrate the darkness.

It is often those who do fear the Lord and obey Him who will be plunged into the darkness of persecution. As Matthew says, a servant is not above his master (see Matt. 10:24). We know that Jesus went through extremes of suffering that His followers will never have to face. He took upon Himself our sin and was crucified in our place. He went through the darkness of Gethsemane and of Calvary. He warned His followers that they would be persecuted. In recent months we have had news of Christians being persecuted in China, in Eritrea, in Sri Lanka, in Turkey, in Bangladesh, in Iraq and in many other parts of the world. We can truly say that they are walking in the dark. But the Lord invites them to trust in Him and rely on Him. As Simon Peter once said to Jesus: 'Lord, to whom shall we go? You have the words of eternal life' (John 6:68). He is the One to turn to.

Let your light shine

1. Have you ever faced persecution – or mockery or criticism – because you profess to follow Jesus? How would you respond to this kind of suffering?
2. If you are not informed about the way Christians in different parts of the world are being persecuted, you could sign up to receive news from Christian organisations that are seeking to support those who are suffering in this way – for example, Open Doors (www.opendoorsuk.org) or Barnabas Fund (www.barnabasfund.org).

Light to live by
Pray for the persecuted Church.

13 Dec

Light will rise

Light for your path

> Even in darkness light dawns for the upright,
>   for the gracious and compassionate and righteous man.
>
>   Psalm 112:4

> ... your light will break forth like the dawn ...
> then your righteousness will go before you ...
> if you spend yourselves on behalf of the hungry
>   and satisfy the needs of the oppressed,
> then your light will rise in the darkness,
>   and your night will become like the noonday.
>
>   Isaiah 58:8,10

Once again the psalmist and the prophet express very similar thoughts in the two passages we have quoted today. What wonderful hope lies behind those words, 'light dawns', 'your light will break forth like the dawn' and 'your light will rise in the darkness'! Night and darkness will not last forever, but while they do God's people must continue to reflect Him in the way they live. We are considered to be righteous in God's eyes because of the imputed righteousness of Jesus Christ (see Rom. 5:18–19). It is as if we were clothed in His righteousness. In fact, Paul tells the Christians in Rome to 'clothe [themselves] with the Lord Jesus Christ' (Rom. 13:14). God has blessed us; we in turn must be a blessing to others. Our lives should be a testimony to what God has done for us. Acts of mercy and kindness and generosity help to dispel the darkness and enable the light to shine. In today's selection of verses we move metaphorically through darkness to the light of dawn and on to the brightness of the noonday sun.

Shedding light

In the part of France where I live – just over the border from Geneva, Switzerland – we spend a good part of the winter under low cloud and murky, damp fog. Outside of the relatively small 'Geneva basin', other people enjoy bright skies and sunshine. The word 'basin' explains it all: bad weather is funnelled to the end of Lake Geneva and it just hangs there. But the lake is not the only physical feature in the immediate area. Geneva is also surrounded by mountains: the Jura to the west, the Alps to the southeast, and two smaller ranges, the Voirons and the Salève. On foggy days, who could ever imagine the breathtaking sight of the Mont Blanc, culminating at 4,800 metres, its snowy white peak etched against an intense blue sky? The fog completely obliterates all such beauty and majesty. However, that does not change the fact that up there, with the sun shining all around, the Mont Blanc rises in all its splendour. We know it is there; we believe it is, even though it is hidden from our eyes.

On a gloomy grey day we have often driven the few kilometres needed in order to leave the cold, dark, clammy fog behind and enter a world of light. What a contrast! We feel alive! We can really breathe again as we drink deeply of the fresh, clean air. We experience warmth as we lift our faces to the caressing rays of the sun. Our stiff, heavy limbs are invigorated as we step out freely and joyfully in the brightness.

It is like living in two different worlds: the darkness 'down here' and the luminous transparency 'up there'. Our lives on earth are often clouded by fear, pain, sorrow or uncertainty. All seems dark. However, despite the dimness and fog, God's promises remain true. His light shines in the darkness.

Let your light shine

1. Reflect on the hope expressed by the words 'light dawns' and 'your light will break forth like the dawn' and 'your light will rise in the darkness'. What practical acts of yours could prove the truth of these words?
2. How would you define 'a righteous man'?
3. What is the antidote to fearing bad news?
4. How can you live this life in the light of eternity?

Light to live by
Thank You, Lord, that You see me as righteous in Jesus Christ. Help me to reflect Him in the way I live. I confess, Lord, that I am often fearful. Help me to trust You completely so that my heart will be steadfast and confident.

14 Dec

Everlasting light

Light for your path

> 'Arise, shine, for your light has come,
>   and the glory of the LORD rises upon you.
> See, darkness covers the earth
>   and thick darkness is over the peoples,
> but the LORD rises upon you
>   and his glory appears over you.
> Nations will come to your light,
>   and kings to the brightness of your dawn ...
> The sun will no more be your light by day,
>   nor will the brightness of the moon shine on you,
> for the LORD will be your everlasting light,
>   and your God will be your glory.
> Your sun will never set again,
>   and your moon will wane no more;
> the LORD will be your everlasting light,
> and your days of sorrow will end.
>
> Isaiah 60:1–3,19–20

You may have noticed that biblical prophecies often refer to more than one event at a time. They sometimes have an immediate historical fulfilment, but can also point to something in the future that has not yet taken place. For this reason prophecies are not always easy to understand and interpret. In today's verses Isaiah is writing primarily about the return from exile, but some of his language reminds us of expressions in the book of Revelation and could be applied to the 'new Jerusalem'. Isaiah sees the world as being covered in darkness, depicting times of oppression and sin. In fact he uses the term 'thick darkness' to express the evil perpetrated by people. It reminds me of an expression I read in Jude's letter the morning I wrote this. Jude refers to 'godless men' (Jude 4) 'for whom blackest darkness has been reserved for ever' (Jude 13). Proverbs 4:19 talks of 'deep darkness'. '*Thick* darkness', '*blackest* darkness', '*deep* darkness' (my italics) emphasise the extent of sin and evil and the severity of judgment.

However, by contrast, Jerusalem is lit up with the Lord's glory. The Lord Himself is its light. This light does not just shine on the city, but God's people themselves radiate His glory; they shine too. Nations will be attracted to the light. Unbelievers will be drawn to God because of His light reflected in His people. Darkness gives way to the brightness of dawn. In the same way the thick darkness is dispelled by the light of God's glory. Much later, describing the 'new Jerusalem', John says 'It shone with the glory of God' (Rev. 21:11) and 'The city does not need the sun or the moon to shine on it, for the glory of God gives it light ...' (Rev. 21:23).

Shedding light
Surely the Church should be the same kind of beacon. We – members of God's Church – should be shining so brightly that unbelievers are attracted to Him. We have already referred to Matthew's words: '... let your light shine before men, that they may see your good deeds and praise your Father in heaven' (Matt. 5:16). Our light will be more visible when we are together. Last year on Christmas Eve about thirty of us from our church opened up the church premises and provided a meal for anyone in the area who was alone. Outside night had fallen; it was dark. A small gift and an invitation were offered to people on the streets. Altogether about ten 'strangers' – ranging from a tramp who was living on the streets by choice, to immigrants looking for work, to people who were simply lonely – joined us for all or part of our evening's celebration. We ate together, had plenty of opportunity to chat, then at the approach to midnight we sang carols and had some readings pointing to the One who is the Light of the world. Each newcomer was given a New

Testament as the evening drew to a close. We pray that God's Word will illumine their lives.

Let your light shine

1. Why not go out one morning and watch the sunrise? See the darkness change to light and rejoice in the light of God's glory.
2. In what ways might your church be more effective in radiating God's glory?

Light to live by

Lord, as Your people, we want to radiate Your glory. We want to shine so that people will be attracted to You. We pray that Your Church will be lit up with Your glory and that many more people will come to put their trust in You.

1. Alec Motyer, *The Prophecy of Isaiah* (Leicester: IVP, 1993) p.98.
2. Verse from 'Light has dawned' used with permission.
3. Michael Green, *The Message of Matthew, The Bible Speaks Today* series (Leicester: IVP, 2000) p.92.
4. Beryl Adamsbaum, *Paths of Peace* (Farnham: CWR, 2007) p.184.

From Darkness to Light

Having looked mainly at passages from the Old Testament during the first two weeks of this month, we now turn primarily to the New Testament and particularly to the Gospels for this week's readings. We will see that many of the Old Testament prophecies were fulfilled when Jesus came into the world. Just before healing a man who was in darkness because he had been born blind, Jesus said: 'While I am in the world, I am the light of the world' (John 9:5). The man testified to the transformation that had come upon him: 'I was blind but now I see!' (John 9:25). The light had a positive effect on him. In the recent film *Amazing Grace*, we hear John Newton use those same words to reflect his own spiritual transformation. Jesus used this physical healing to teach a lesson about spiritual blindness. Those – like the Pharisees who challenged Jesus – who claimed they could see but were in fact content to stay in the dark, would bear the consequences of their sin. Let us make sure that we follow Jesus, so that we will have 'the light of life' and 'never walk in darkness' (see John 8:12).

Amazing grace – how sweet the sound –
that saved a wretch like me!
I once was lost, but now am found,
was blind but now I see.

'Twas grace that taught my heart to fear,
And grace my fears relieved;
How precious did that grace appear
The hour I first believed!

Through many dangers, toils and snares
I have already come;
'Tis grace hath brought me safe thus far,
And grace will lead me home.

John Newton (1725–1807)

The rising sun

Light for your path

'And you, my child, will be called a prophet of the Most High;
    for you will go on before the Lord to prepare the way for him,
to give his people the knowledge of salvation
    through the forgiveness of their sins,
 because of the tender mercy of our God,
    by which the rising sun will come to us from heaven
to shine on those living in darkness
    and in the shadow of death,
to guide our feet into the path of peace.'

Luke 1:76–79

Elizabeth has given birth to John the Baptist. His father, Zechariah, says that he 'will be called a prophet of the Most High'. Leon Morris reminds us that 'there had been no prophet among the Jews for centuries,'[1] so John was to have a radical, key role. He was 'to prepare the way' for the Lord. He would be the forerunner of the Messiah. He would point the way to the Saviour, the One who would forgive the sins of the people. The sun is about to rise. The apostle John says of John the Baptist: 'He came as a witness to testify concerning that light, so that through him all men might believe. He himself was not the light; he came only as a witness to the light. The true light that gives light to every man was coming into the world' (John 1:7–9). Zechariah too speaks of salvation in terms of light that would shine on those living in darkness and lead them 'into the path of peace'. Advent is a time when we can ponder anew 'the tender mercy of our God' and thank Him for the One who came to be our Saviour.

Shedding light

Last Christmas we received our first Christmas card at the end of
November, together with a message that fits well with the theme of this
Advent book: 'If there weren't a Christmas, we'd have to invent one!
Especially in England, where we had the most dismal summer, full of
grey skies and coldness.'[2] Throughout Advent they poured in – not
only cards, but also newsletters and electronic greetings. It was as if
they were preparing the way for the celebration of the Saviour's birth
later in the month. Some of them depicted wise men from the east
following the star which would lead them to 'the one who has been
born king of the Jews' (see Matt. 2:1–2). Others showed 'shepherds
living out in the fields ... keeping watch over their flocks at night', as
related in Luke's Gospel, chapter 2 and verse 8. Then there was the
scene in Bethlehem with 'Mary and Joseph, and the baby, who was
lying in the manger' (Luke 2:16). In keeping with Zechariah's message
of light and peace, most of the pictures on our Christmas cards show
some form of light: stars shining at night, and particularly the star
that the Magi followed; or candles representing Jesus, the Light of the
world. Some of the cards convey a message of peace: 'Peace on earth',
or 'Glory to God in the highest, and on earth peace' (Luke 2:14).

Let your light shine

1. John the Baptist obviously had an exclusive role as the forerunner
   of the Messiah, but in what ways could you also point people to
   the Saviour?
2. How do you prepare to celebrate Christmas?
3. Zechariah concludes his prophetic song with a message of peace
   (see Luke 1:79). How do you relate to that message of peace?
   According to Leon Morris, it refers to 'that peace of God that
   calm's men's hearts and makes them strong to live for God. It
   "does not mean merely freedom from trouble; it means all that
   makes for a man's highest good" (Barclay).'[3]

Light to live by

Ask the Lord to show you creative ways in which you could point
people to the Saviour. Pray for the people whom the Lord lays on
your heart. Pray that 'the rising sun will ... guide [their] feet into the
path of peace.'

16 Dec

A light

Light for your path

> Now there was a man in Jerusalem called Simeon, who was
> righteous and devout. He was waiting for the consolation of
> Israel, and the Holy Spirit was upon him. It had been revealed
> to him by the Holy Spirit that he would not die before he had
> seen the Lord's Christ. Moved by the Spirit, he went into the
> temple courts. When the parents brought in the child Jesus ...
> Simeon took him in his arms and praised God, saying:
>
> 'Sovereign Lord, as you have promised,
>   you now dismiss your servant in peace.
> For my eyes have seen your salvation,
>   which you have prepared in the sight of all people,
> a light for revelation to the Gentiles
>   and for glory to your people Israel.'
>
> Luke 2:25–32

Nothing is known about Simeon apart from Luke's reference to him. We
tend to think he must have been old, because he said he was ready to
die, but we are not actually told his age. Some people think he must
have been a priest because he was in the Temple courts, but Luke
doesn't actually say so. What we do know is that he was 'righteous and
devout' and that he was waiting for the Messiah ('the consolation of
Israel') to come. It would seem as if 'the Holy Spirit was upon him' in a
special way. The Holy Spirit had made it clear to him that he would see
'the Lord's Christ' before he died. It was this same Spirit who prompted
him to go into the Temple courts just when Joseph and Mary were
bringing in Jesus in accordance with 'the custom of the Law' (v.27). And
what Simeon had been waiting for came to pass: he saw with his own
eyes the Saviour of the world. Luke makes it clear that Jesus had come
not just for the nation of Israel, but for the Gentiles too. He was 'a light
for revelation to the Gentiles and for glory to your people Israel.' And
yet following Simeon's song of praise to God, we discern – along with

the light – a theme of darkness too. He concludes on a sombre note by saying to Mary: '... a sword will pierce your own soul ...' (Luke 2:35). In these few verses, Luke evokes the darkness and anguish of the cross as well as the light and joy of the incarnation.

Shedding light

How many of us – when meditating on the crucifixion – spend any time dwelling on Mary's pain and suffering? What agony she must have endured to see her Son put to death. Simeon's prophecy was realised thirty years later when Mary's soul was indeed torn and pierced. Some of you reading this book may have been bereaved during Advent or at Christmas one year. Amid the general rejoicing, your soul was pierced. You are experiencing the 'dark night of the soul'. A personal note on a Christmas card we once received revealed the devastation and intense loneliness of a friend who lost his wife just under a year before. As I write this my own sister is devotedly and agonisingly nursing her husband through his last days on earth. If Simeon was waiting for 'the consolation of Israel', we know that the consolation and comfort did come.

And we know that beyond the darkness of Calvary shines the bright light of the resurrection. There is hope for the future. There is light at the end of the tunnel.

Let your light shine

1. Read the whole passage (Luke 2:21–35) to get more background and further details regarding this incident concerning Simeon.
2. Luke says that 'the child's father and mother marvelled at what was said about him' (Luke 2:33). Spend time meditating and marvelling at what you know about Jesus – His birth, His childhood, His ministry, His death and resurrection and ascension and the fact that He will come again.

Light to live by

Thank the Lord that He came to be your Saviour. Thank Him that He came to be the Saviour of the world – for both Jews and Gentiles. Praise God that many people throughout the world have turned to Him. Pray that more and more people will hear and understand the message of salvation and put their trust in Christ.

17 Dec

The light of the world

Light for your path

... Jesus ... said, 'I am the light of the world. Whoever follows me will never walk in darkness, but will have the light of life.'

John 8:12

'As long as it is day, we must do the work of him who sent me. Night is coming, when no-one can work. While I am in the world, I am the light of the world.'

John 9:4–5

We have already referred briefly to these words of Jesus more than once. In John's Gospel chapter 8, Jesus is in Jerusalem for the festival of Tabernacles. During the feast a golden candelabra was lit in memory of the pillar of light in the sky that guided the people of Israel through the desert. Jesus may have used this ceremony of lights as a springboard for declaring Himself to be 'the light of the world' that gives illumination to His followers. It is the healing of the man born blind in John chapter 9 that reveals to us something of the nature of this light. 'This miracle is a sign that Jesus can open the eyes of the spiritually blind so that they can receive the complete sight which constitutes perfect faith. Faith means passing from darkness to light ...'[4] Jesus was born into a world, which according to Isaiah's prophecy was full of 'distress and darkness and fearful gloom' (Isa. 8:22). How wonderful, then, to be able to follow Jesus, the light of the world, and to claim His promise that we 'will never walk in darkness, but will have the light of life'.

Shedding light

We couldn't have a better application for these verses than the words of this wonderful hymn:

The whole world was lost in the darkness of sin,
The Light of the world is Jesus;

Like sunshine at noonday His glory shone in,
The Light of the world is Jesus.

Chorus:
Come to the Light, 'tis shining for thee;
Sweetly the Light has dawn'd upon me,
Once I was blind but now I can see;
The Light of the world is Jesus.

No darkness have we who in Jesus abide,
The Light of the world is Jesus,
We walk in the light when we follow our Guide,
The Light of the world is Jesus.

Ye dwellers in darkness, with sin-blinded eyes,
The Light of the world is Jesus,
Go, wash at his bidding, and light will arise,
The Light of the world is Jesus.

No need of the sunlight in heaven, we're told;
The Light of that world is Jesus;
The Lamb is the Light in the City of Gold,
The Light of that world is Jesus.

P.P. Bliss (1838–1876)

Let your light shine
1. Read the whole of John chapter 9 to see how Jesus healed the man born blind and how He used this incident to teach about spiritual blindness.
2. How can we point those who are walking in darkness – the darkness of sin or sorrow or pain or deprivation – to the One who is the Light of the world?

Light to live by
Pray for those you know who are walking in darkness. Pray that their lives will be transformed by an encounter with Jesus the Light of the world and that they will pass from darkness to light.

18 Dec

Light in the darkness

Light for your path

> In the beginning was the Word, and the Word was with God,
> and the Word was God. He was with God in the beginning.
> Through him all things were made; without him nothing was
> made that has been made. In him was life, and that life was the
> light of men. The light shines in the darkness, but the darkness
> has not understood it ...
> The true light that gives light to every man was coming into
> the world.
>
> John 1:1–5,9

God reveals Himself primarily through His Son, the living Word. It is
He who is the source of light. And He gives us life. The life that is
mentioned here is not just physical life, but spiritual life too, which John
qualifies as 'light'. We know that God's world, which He saw to be 'very
good' when He created it (Gen. 1:31), has been spoiled by sin, and that
men and women whom He created in His own image (Gen. 1:27) have
sinned. The image is no longer a true likeness. 'But, however gross the
darkness may be, the Light of the divine Word shines on and is not
obliterated.'[5] 'It is the function of light to shine precisely in the darkness,
to oppose darkness, to dispel darkness ... Jesus' whole mission was
a conflict between the light and the darkness.'[6] It is interesting and
significant that at the beginning of his Gospel, John writes in the past
tense until he mentions the light. 'The light shines' is in the present
tense. It shines now and always. It triumphs over the darkness.

Verse 9 (above) – 'The true light ... was coming into the world' –
refers of course to the incarnation, the Word becoming flesh, which
is exactly what we will be celebrating in a week's time. Jesus is 'the
true light', the real Light, the genuine Light, the Light that gives light
– real illumination – to people.

Shedding light
One elderly American friend from whom we heard last Christmas

remarked how hard it is to keep a positive attitude while the world crumbles around us. However, amid the gloom and doom, she recognises that Christ never changes. The Light still shines in the darkness. She gleans hope from the fact that He is in control. The writer of the letter to the Hebrews tells us clearly and categorically that 'Jesus Christ is the same yesterday and today and forever' (Heb. 13:8). What an encouraging, reassuring statement! What a wonderful truth to hold onto in a rapidly changing world!

Let your light shine
1. In what way is Jesus 'the true light that gives light to every man' (John 1:9)?
2. How will you celebrate 'the true light … coming into the world'?
3. What does it mean to you to know that Jesus never changes?

Light to live by

Christ, whose glory fills the skies,
Christ, the true, the only Light,
Sun of Righteousness, arise,
Triumph o'er the shades of night!
Day-spring from on high, be near!
Day-star in my heart appear!

Dark and cheerless is the morn
Unaccompanied by Thee;
Joyless is the day's return,
Till Thy mercy's beams I see;
Till they inward light impart,
Glad my eyes, and warm my heart.

Visit then this soul of mine,
Pierce the gloom of sin and grief!
Fill me, Radiancy Divine,
Scatter all my unbelief!
More and more Thyself display,
Shining to the perfect day!

Charles Wesley (1707–1788)

19 Dec

Light and truth

Light for your path

> '... Light has come into the world, but men loved darkness
> instead of light because their deeds were evil. Everyone who
> does evil hates the light, and will not come into the light for
> fear that his deeds will be exposed. But whoever lives by the
> truth comes into the light, so that it may be seen plainly that
> what he has done has been done through God.'
>
> John 3:19–21

Five times in these few lines John mentions the word 'light'. It is
obviously an important concept. Light and darkness in this passage
are closely related to good and evil. Though, when he says, 'Light
has come into the world,' surely John also has in mind the fact that
Jesus, 'the light of the world', has come to earth.

At the beginning of John chapter 3, Jesus has in fact been talking
with Nicodemus. (You can read the whole of their conversation
in John 3:1–21.) Actually, as we get to the end of this passage, it
is not certain if Jesus is still speaking or whether John himself is
reflecting on the meaning of Jesus' words. Jesus has just explained
to Nicodemus what it means to be 'born again' (v.3). Nicodemus
– 'Israel's teacher' (v.10) – has trouble getting his mind around the
spiritual meaning of Jesus' words. Jesus explains that He – God's
Son – has come into the world 'to save the world' (v.17). Those who
believe are saved; those who do not believe are condemned. Jesus
uses the analogy of light and darkness to emphasise His teaching.
Those who are condemned have made their choice: they prefer
darkness to light. They refuse the light, so that their 'evil deeds' will
remain hidden in the darkness. Implicitly, if they reject the light, they
not only refuse to do good, but they also reject the One who is 'the
light of the world'.

Shedding light

Solomon beautifully describes this same dichotomy between light and darkness, or good and evil, or righteousness and wickedness. In Proverbs chapter 4 he says: 'The path of the righteous is like the first gleam of dawn, shining ever brighter till the full light of day. But the way of the wicked is like deep darkness; they do not know what makes them stumble' (vv.18–19). In our text for today the people concerned are confronted with a choice. They have a moral decision to make. They are responsible human beings. They can choose darkness or light. Their condemnation stems from the fact that they prefer the darkness. In fact John uses a very strong word when he says that they *hate* the light. They do not want their evil deeds to be seen. By contrast, 'whoever lives by the truth comes into the light,' says John. 'Whoever lives by the truth' is a person who sincerely wants to live out the truth of God's Word, who wants to live in a way that is pleasing to God, who wants to do what is right and whose behaviour is transparent. God has created us all to be responsible. We are responsible for our own choices and decisions and actions. Remember those words of Moses that we quoted earlier: '... choose life, so that you ... may live ...' (Deut. 30:19).

Let your light shine

1. It is not up to us to judge whether any given person has chosen darkness or light, but how can we help people recognise their responsibility to choose wisely and morally?
2. Examine your heart before God to see whether you would honestly choose darkness or light, knowing that your 'deeds will be exposed' in the light.
3. What does it mean to you personally to live by the truth?

Light to live by

> Search me, O God, and know my heart;
>   test me and know my anxious thoughts.
> See if there is any offensive way in me,
>   and lead me in the way everlasting.

Psalm 139:23–24

20 Dec

Trust in the light

Light for your path

> Then Jesus told them, 'You are going to have the light just
> a little while longer. Walk while you have the light, before
> darkness overtakes you. The man who walks in the dark does
> not know where he is going. Put your trust in the light while
> you have it, so that you may become sons of light ...
> I have come into the world as a light, so that no-one who
> believes in me should stay in darkness.'
>
> John 12:35–36,46

Jesus is in conversation with a 'crowd' (v.34). Basically He is telling
them to change their thinking and to act upon what He is saying,
to act upon the light they have. What does He mean when He says,
'Put your trust in the light while you have it'? Surely, implicitly,
Jesus is saying that He Himself is the light. He will not be with them
much longer. He will soon leave this world. 'He who came into the
world as the light which enlightens every man was about to leave
it through the darkness of the cross.'⁷ If they do not act now, the
light will fade and disappear. It is not easy to find one's way in the
dark. In the light we see clearly; in darkness we might get lost. 'Walk
while you have the light,' says Jesus. He wants us to put our trust in
Him and so become 'sons of light', so that our whole being will be
illuminated by Him and will reflect Him.

Shedding light

On New Year's Eve last year we were invited to visit some friends in
their new home in France and to stay overnight so that we wouldn't
be travelling home in the dark. The house they have bought is in
quite an isolated area in a part of the country we do not know
very well. For that reason, they also kindly agreed to our arriving in
daylight rather than after nightfall, so that we wouldn't get lost on
our way there. It is so much easier to find one's way in the light!
This is what Jesus says too in today's passage. At this time of the

year night falls early in the northern hemisphere. As it turned out, weather conditions and road conditions were so bad at the end of last year that we unfortunately had to cancel our plans. Jesus says that the light will not last much longer. 'Walk while you have the light, before darkness overtakes you.' There seems to be an urgency about His words. Time is short. Night is coming. We must act – and act now, before it is too late. Our text today is really an appeal to trust Jesus. If you haven't yet put your trust in Him, do it now!

Let your light shine
1. What does Jesus mean when He says, 'The man who walks in the dark does not know where he is going'?
2. Do you get the impression that you are walking in the dark or in the light? Why?
3. Would you say that you know where you are going? Can you explain where you are going?
4. Have you 'put your trust in the light'? If so, what difference has it made in your life? If not, why not do so now?

Light to live by
Thank You, Lord, that You came into the world as a light, so that no one who believes in You should stay in darkness. Thank You for Your invitation to put my trust in You, You who are the Light of the world. Thank You for going through the darkness of Calvary so that I might have the light of life.

21 Dec

Full of light

Light for your path

'The eye is the lamp of the body. If your eyes are good, your whole body will be full of light. But if your eyes are bad, your whole body will be full of darkness. If then the light within you is darkness, how great is that darkness!'

Matthew 6:22–23

In order to understand these words of Jesus, we need to see them in their context. Jesus is teaching His disciples. He has already spoken to them about various subjects. Now He is talking to them basically about money. If you have the time, read the whole passage: Matthew 6:19–24. Jesus is explaining that we have to choose, in fact, between God and money. There can be no divided loyalties. God must come first. He encourages His followers to make sure that they 'store up for [themselves] treasures in heaven' (v.20). This is the only treasure that will last.

In our verses for today, Jesus talks first of all about 'the eye'. Eyes can tell us quite a lot about a person. By looking at a person's eyes, we can see happiness or sadness. We might perceive a puzzled look. We see hardness or else a look of love or compassion. 'The eye is the lamp of the body,' says Jesus. R.V.G. Tasker comments: 'The eyes were looked upon by the ancients as the windows through which light entered the body. If the eyes were therefore in good condition the whole body was lit up and receptive of the benefits that light can bestow; but if the eyes were bad the whole body was plunged in the darkness that breeds disease.'[8]

So, if the eyes were good, the person's life would be completely focused on God. And the lesson Jesus is trying to get across is the following: 'You cannot be devoted to God if you are devoted to money and the things money will buy.'[9]

Shedding light
This teaching of Jesus really helps us to get our priorities right. In the general commotion and confusion during these weeks preceding Christmas, money and spending tend to have a key role. Let us not fall into the trap of materialism. Without going into any detail about the amount we might spend on food, drinks and presents – not to mention Christmas trees, lights and decorations – maybe we could decide to simplify a little. At the same time we want to be warm-hearted and generous to our loved ones, and also – as we have opportunity – to those in need. In our spending, as in all areas of life, we need wisdom and discernment and we need to have our priorities firmly in place.

The financial crisis has certainly curtailed spending. Maybe it will help us to think things through, reassess our priorities, draw some conclusions and reach out in love and compassion.

Let your light shine

1. Do you tend to look people in the eye when they speak to you? What do you see when you do?
2. Explain in your own words what you think Jesus means when He says, 'The eye is the lamp of the body ...' (Matt. 6:22).
3. What are your priorities in life? Where is your 'treasure'? (See Matthew 6:21.)

Light to live by

At this time of the year there are many relief organisations – both Christian and secular – in different countries distributing meals to those in need. Pray that the love and the light of Christ will shine through those who are doing this in His name, and that needy people everywhere will be drawn to Him.

Dear Lord, help me to get my priorities right. Give me wisdom and discernment as far as spending goes. Help me to manage my funds. I want to put You first, Lord. Show me how You want me to help those who lack some of the basic necessities of life.

1. Leon Morris, *Luke, an Introduction and Commentary* (London: IVP, 1974) p.80.
2. Muriel Weisz, quoted with permission.
3. Leon Morris, *Luke, an Introduction and Commentary* (London: IVP, 1974) p.81.
4. R.V.G. Tasker, *John, an Introduction and Commentary* (London: Tyndale Press, 1968) pp.122–123.
5. Ibid., p.43.
6. Leon Morris, *The Gospel according to John* (Grand Rapids, Michigan: Eerdmans, 1971) p.84.
7. Merrill C. Tenney, *John, the Gospel of Belief* (Grand Rapids, Michigan: Eerdmans, 1948) p.190.
8. R.V.G.Tasker, *Matthew, an Introduction and Commentary* (London: The Tyndale Press, 1969) p.75.
9. Michael Green, *The message of Matthew* (Leicester: IVP, 2000) p.103.

The Light of the Gospel

We move on this week to consider passages from some of the
New Testament letters. In the Gospels we saw that Jesus came
into the world as the Light of the world. There was much rejoicing
at His birth. We saw how 'the glory of the Lord' shone around the
shepherds in the fields (see Luke 2:8–14). We also saw how Jesus
is introduced in John's Gospel as the Light shining in the darkness.
Some people turn to Him for life and salvation, but others remain
lost in the darkness of sin. We know that Jesus was born to die.
The darkness of Calvary was the fulfilment of His earthly mission.
But Jesus rose from the dead! He was victorious over the grave!
He broke the power of sin! He is now 'seated at the right hand
of God' (Col. 3:1), but He is coming back again in glory, and we
know that 'we will be with the Lord for ever' (1 Thess. 4:17). In the
meantime, we have His Spirit living within us, to guide us into all
truth (see John 16:13). We try to follow Jesus; we try to 'walk in
the light'. Sometimes we fall. How wonderful to be able to turn
to Him in repentance and count on His forgiveness. He does not
give up on us.

Wait till the Lord comes

Light for your path

> ... judge nothing before the appointed time; wait till the Lord comes. He will bring to light what is hidden in darkness and will expose the motives of men's hearts. At that time each will receive his praise from God.
>
> 1 Corinthians 4:5

The apostle Paul is writing to the Christians in Corinth about judgment. He says that only God can judge correctly, so there is not much point in passing judgment on one another. They should stop doing this. In fact, God who knows people's hearts will judge perfectly. 'He will bring to light what is hidden in darkness ...' 'Darkness' here is probably used in the sense of evil. Paul says that hidden evil motives will be brought to light and exposed. If some people act according to good and pure motives, God will praise them for that. He alone knows our hearts. He alone is just. In one of his letters to Timothy, Paul refers to God as 'the Lord, the righteous Judge' (2 Tim. 4:8).

Shedding light

How sad that in so many parts of the world people are not only passing judgment on one another, but are taking judgment into their own hands, on a personal level and at a national level too. Innocent civilians – families including children – are being killed. Homes are destroyed. As I write this, Israel has recently attacked Gaza in an attempt to annihilate the Hamas movement. The Executive Director of Evangelicals for Middle East Understanding (EMEU) expressed the anguish suffered by those who love all peoples of the Middle

East (Jews, Muslims and Christians). He sent us a written report from one Israeli rabbi whose heart went out to the Palestinians who were suffering undeservedly. Paradoxically this was taking place during Hanukkah, the Jewish Festival of Lights.

At the same time we received a letter from some Lebanese friends, thrilled that after previous dark days, Beirut was once again illuminated by Christmas lights and decorations. They sent a photograph to prove it!

'Wait till the Lord comes', says our text. Well, the Lord came. And He will come again. The 'light of the world' shone in the darkness of a sinful world. He said, 'I did not come to judge the world, but to save it' (John 12:47). The invitation is open to all. As Philip Bliss says in that beautiful hymn we quoted last week, 'Come to the Light, 'tis shining for thee ...'

Let your light shine

1. Jesus said, 'As long as it is day, we must do the work of him who sent me. Night is coming, when no-one can work' (John 9:4). What work do you think the Lord wants you to do for Him?

2. The Executive Director of Evangelicals for Middle East Understanding is also President of Venture International, a Christian organisation working in the Middle East and Central Asia. You can find out more about how these organisations are involved in helping needy people in these parts of the world by consulting their respective websites: www.emeu.net and www.ventureint.org

Light to live by

Pray for the Middle East. Pray for peace. Pray for those who are involved in bringing relief to people in need. Pray that refugees and those who have been injured or bereaved will not be overcome by the darkness of their situation but will 'come to the light'.

23 Dec

God's light in our hearts

Light for your path

The god of this age has blinded the minds of unbelievers, so
that they cannot see the light of the gospel of the glory of
Christ, who is the image of God ... For God, who said, 'Let light
shine out of darkness,' made his light shine in our hearts to give
us the light of the knowledge of the glory of God in the face of
Christ.

2 Corinthians 4:4,6

'The god of this age' – Satan, the devil – does his best to stop people
turning to Christ, to the point of blinding their minds and preventing
them from seeing 'the light of the gospel of the glory of Christ'. Later
in the same letter Paul says that Satan 'masquerades as an angel of
light' (2 Cor. 11:14). He is not what he makes himself out to be.
He is disguised. We must not let ourselves be taken in by him. Not
all light is what it seems to be. With reference to the attacks on
Gaza that we mentioned yesterday, one BBC reporter was struck by
the way the night sky of Gaza was illuminated with the light from
bombs.

We rejoice that God can deliver those whose minds have been
blinded by the devil. In his first letter to the Christians in Colosse,
Paul says that he gives 'thanks to the Father, who has qualified you
to share in the inheritance of the saints in the kingdom of light. For
he has rescued us from the dominion of darkness' (Col. 1:12–14).
Paul reminds us here of a fact we referred to in the introduction to
Week One of this book, namely that 'at the dawn of creation the
darkness was dispelled by the word of Almighty God (see Gen.
1:2f.); and it is the same God who, in the spiritual sphere, drives
back the darkness of sin and unbelief from the hearts of men'.[1] In
fact, Paul is probably thinking back to his own conversion on the
Damascus road, when he saw 'a light from heaven, brighter than the
sun, blazing around me and my companions' (Acts 26:13).

Shedding light

The apostle Paul had a dramatic conversion experience, which you can read about in Acts 9:1–20. Prior to this he had been involved in persecuting the Early Church (see Acts 8:3). He was actually on his way to Damascus to take the Christians there as prisoners to Jerusalem when 'a light from heaven flashed around him. He fell to the ground and heard a voice say to him, "Saul, Saul, why do you persecute me?"' (Acts 9:3–4). He discovered that it was Jesus speaking to him. When he got up, he was blind. The Lord told him what to do and where to go and He sent Ananias to restore his sight. From that time on Paul was transformed and began to preach that 'Jesus is the Son of God' (Acts 9:20).

How encouraging to read that one who had once been 'breathing out murderous threats against the Lord's disciples' (Acts 9:1), later began to follow the Lord himself and became a Christian leader and the author of a large part of the New Testament. In spite of Satan's ploys, Paul came to 'see the light of the gospel of the glory of Christ'. Let us not be discouraged when people around us and particularly family members whom we love, still seem to be blind to the truth of the gospel. Let us keep praying for them, and let us take courage from the experience and example of the apostle Paul.

Let your light shine

1. Like the apostle Paul, look back on your own conversion experience. How would you describe what happened to you then?
2. What do you find particularly encouraging about Paul's experience?
3. Under what circumstances and in what way could you best apply the following exhortation: 'Be self-controlled and alert. Your enemy the devil prowls around like a roaring lion looking for someone to devour. Resist him, standing firm in the faith ...' (1 Pet. 5:8–9).

Light to live by

Thank You, Lord, for rescuing me 'from the dominion of darkness'. I pray for those whose minds have been blinded by 'the god of this age'. I pray that You will free them from bondage. I pray that the devil will not be allowed to blind their minds any longer, or delude them or deceive them. As we approach Christmas, open their eyes, Lord, to 'see the light of the gospel of the glory of Christ'.

24 Dec

Darkness or light?

Light for your path

> Do not be yoked together with unbelievers. For what do righteousness and wickedness have in common? Or what fellowship can light have with darkness? What harmony is there between Christ and Belial? What does a believer have in common with an unbeliever? What agreement is there between the temple of God and idols? For we are the temple of the living God. As God has said: 'I will live with them and walk among them, and I will be their God, and they will be my people.'
>
> 'Therefore come out from them and be separate,
>   says the Lord.'
>
> 2 Corinthians 6:14–17

I often think that living the Christian life is like walking a tightrope. It is not easy to be 'in the world' but 'not of the world' (John 17:11,14). It is not easy to frequent sinners without falling into sin. It is not easy to draw alongside immoral people without being influenced by them or identifying with their evil ways. And yet Paul's exhortation is clear: we must be different from unbelievers, as different as light is from darkness. We must not be assimilated into dark areas of unrighteousness. Paul must consider this to be very important otherwise he would not have used so many different expressions and examples to get his teaching across. All his questions expect some form of negative answer. (He uses the name 'Belial' for Satan.) So, by giving all these different examples, he is basically saying that it is impossible for a believer to be 'yoked' with an unbeliever. James endorses Paul's teaching when he says,

'... don't you know that friendship with the world is hatred towards God? Anyone who chooses to be a friend of the world becomes an enemy of God' (James 4:4). As we prepare to celebrate Christmas, the Nativity, the incarnation, God become man in the Person of Jesus Christ, we must decide whose side we are on. We must make a stand. There can be no compromise.

Shedding Light

Who is on the Lord's side?
Who will serve the King?
Who will be His helpers
Other lives to bring?
Who will leave the world's side?
Who will face the foe?
Who is on the Lord's side?
Who for Him will go?

By Thy call of mercy,
By Thy grace divine,
We are on the Lord's side,
Saviour, we are Thine.

Frances Ridley Havergal (1836–1879)

Let your light shine

1. In what specific areas of life could you apply Paul's command not to 'be yoked together with unbelievers'?
2. When the Lord says, '... come out from them and be separate,' what does He mean exactly?
3. How do you apply Paul's analogy of light and darkness to his teaching in today's passage?
4. What are the implications of Paul's words, 'For we are the temple of the living God'?

Light to live by

Thank You, Lord, that when You came into the world You – the sinless One – identified with sinful humanity. Now, Lord, I want to identify with You. I want to make a stand for You and live for You. I thank You, Lord, for the transforming work of Your Spirit within me, making me more like Jesus.

25 Dec – Christmas Day

Wonderful light

Light for your path

> But you are a chosen people, a royal priesthood, a holy nation, a people belonging to God, that you may declare the praises of him who called you out of darkness into his wonderful light.
>
> 1 Peter 2:9

Last week our general theme was 'From darkness to light'. When we find this expression in the Bible, it usually refers to the radical change wrought in the lives of people who have turned from paganism to Christ, from unbelief to belief. When Paul appeared before King Agrippa, he explained to him that God had sent him to both Jews and Gentiles, 'to open their eyes and turn them from darkness to light, and from the power of Satan to God' (Acts 26:18). Peter describes what we became when we moved from darkness to light and took the step of following Jesus: '… a chosen people, a royal priesthood, a holy nation, a people belonging to God …'. He probably picked up these expressions from the Old Testament, where prophecies concerning darkness and light pointed to the One whose birth we celebrate today – Jesus, the Light of the world. Earlier in this book we mentioned the importance of fellowship, of being together. The expressions Peter uses to describe those of us who have been called out of darkness into God's wonderful light would endorse that spirit of community.

Today we celebrate the birth of Jesus, the Light of the world, who called us out of darkness into His wonderful light. That is certainly worth celebrating! In our verse for today, Peter qualifies God's light as 'wonderful', or – as in other versions – 'marvellous'. 'This light is "marvellous", "wonderful"…, not only as evoking our wonder, but even more as exhibiting the wonders of God's power … which we are to proclaim.'² The reason God chose us and called us out of darkness into His wonderful light is so that we too might illuminate the world in which we live and so that we might declare His praises.

Shedding light

Jesus bids us shine
With a pure, clear light;
Like a little candle
Burning in the night.
In this world of darkness
So we must shine –
You in your small corner,
And I in mine.

Jesus bids us shine,
First of all for Him;
Well He sees and knows it
If our light grows dim.
He looks down from heaven
To see us shine –
You in your small corner,
And I in mine.

Jesus bids us shine,
Then, for all around;
Many kinds of darkness
In this world abound –
Sin and want and sorrow;
So we must shine –
You in your small corner,
And I in mine.

Susan Warner (1819–1885)

Let your light shine
1. Why did God call you 'out of darkness into His wonderful light'?
2. What does it mean to you to declare the praises of God? How do you declare His praises?

3. Consider in turn these four expressions, 'a chosen people', 'a royal priesthood', 'a holy nation', 'a people belonging to God'. How does the Church today fit those descriptions?

Light to live by

Thank You, Lord, for taking upon Yourself our humanity and for being born in such humble conditions. Thank You for identifying with those You came to save. Thank You for lighting up our dark world. Thank You for calling us out of darkness into Your wonderful light. I want to praise You, Lord. I want to show forth the wonders of Your power and shine for You in a dark world.

26 Dec

God is light

Light for your path

> ... God is light; in him there is no darkness at all. If we claim to have fellowship with him yet walk in the darkness, we lie and do not live by the truth. But if we walk in the light, as he is in the light, we have fellowship with one another, and the blood of Jesus, his Son, purifies us from all sin.
>
> 1 John 1:5–7

It is amazing really how often we come upon this theme of darkness and light in the Scriptures. It runs throughout the whole Bible, from Genesis to Revelation. It is a key metaphor and teaches us so much about God, about humanity, about good and evil, about truth and error and about the message of salvation and what it means to be a Christian. And how perceptive of John to describe God in this way: 'God is light'. That one word 'light' seems to sum up all the attributes of God. Just as light shines, so God reveals Himself. And, as if that were not enough, just so that his readers will really understand what he is getting at, John qualifies what he has said by adding, 'in him there is no darkness at all'. Light; pure light; ineffable light. Graham Kendrick talks of 'Father's pure radiance'.[3] It follows on naturally that there is no way we could possibly have fellowship with Him if we remain in the darkness of our sins. However, 'if we walk in the light' – purified from all sin by the blood of Jesus, and with our eyes fixed on Him – not only will we have fellowship with God Himself, but we will also have fellowship with other believers.

Shedding light

David Jackman points out that 'if our view of God is distorted, everything else is bound to be out of joint.'[4] That is probably why, right from the outset, John wants to make sure that his readers understand that 'God is light'. If we grasp that much, then surely His light will show up all the dark areas of our own lives. For such a statement obviously has moral implications for us, just as it had for the first recipients of John's letter. We have to choose whether we are going to 'walk' in the light or in darkness. There is no possible means of compromise. It must be one or the other. If we choose to persist in sin, we forfeit fellowship with God. I think John also suggests that if we want to have fellowship with God, we must also have fellowship with other believers. It is normal for a Christian to be part of a local church fellowship, rather than try to live the Christian life alone. 'Christians who live in God's light do not find it difficult to walk together in fellowship. The light shows the way ahead, and enables them to co-ordinate their actions and move forward in harmony.'[5]

Let your light shine

1. What does walking in the light mean to you?
2. Does walking in fellowship with other believers mean that we always agree about everything? How do you handle disagreements? What is the primary meaning of being in fellowship? (See 1 John 3:11; 4:7–21).
3. Do you find it difficult to walk in fellowship with other believers? Why?

Light to live by

Thank You, Jesus, for purifying me from all sin. You make it possible for me to walk in the light. Thank You too for my brothers and sisters in Christ who are also walking in the light and with whom I can have fellowship. May we be an encouragement to one another.

27 Dec

The true light

Light for your path

> ... the darkness is passing and the true light is already shining. Anyone who claims to be in the light but hates his brother is still in the darkness. Whoever loves his brother lives in the light, and there is nothing in him to make him stumble. But whoever hates his brother is in the darkness and walks around in the darkness; he does not know where he is going, because the darkness has blinded him.
>
> 1 John 2:8–11

Commenting on these verses, John Stott says that '*The darkness* is the present age or the "world" ... The *true light*, which *is already shining*, is Jesus Christ. ... the new age ... has been ushered in by the shining of the true light. John now shows that Jesus Christ, the true light, is the light of love ... The light shines on our path, so that we can see clearly and so walk properly.'[6] So in this passage the apostle John is comparing darkness with hatred, and light with love. He paints a vivid picture of a person who hates his brother, stumbling around blindly in the darkness. By contrast, 'whoever loves his brother lives in the light, and there is nothing in him to make him stumble'. It is no good claiming to be in the light if we do not love our fellow Christians. Loving one another is extremely important, because Jesus commands it. Shortly before going to the cross, He said to His disciples: 'This is my command: Love each other' (John 15:17).

Shedding light

Benazir Bhutto died on this day (27 December) in 2007 in an act of terrorism that plunged Pakistan into the darkness of grief and despair. Surely this is an example of the darkness John refers to in his letter. It is a characteristic of what the Bible calls 'this age' (Matt. 12:32) or 'the world' (1 John 2:15). John also makes it clear that 'He who does what is sinful is of the devil' (1 John 3:8). He goes on to say, 'Anyone who does not do what is right is not a child of God; nor is anyone who does not love his brother' (3:10). He gives the example of Cain 'who belonged to the evil one and murdered his brother' (3:12). Christians should be different: 'We should love one another' (1 John 3:11). This theme continues throughout his letter: 'Dear friends, let us love one another, for love comes from God. Everyone who loves has been born of God and knows God. Whoever does not love does not know God, because God is love. This is how God showed his love among us: He sent his one and only Son into the world that we might live through him. This is love: not that we loved God, but that he loved us and sent his Son as an atoning sacrifice for our sins. Dear friends, since God so loved us, we also ought to love one another' (4:7–11).

Let your light shine

1. How did God show His love to us?
2. Jesus' words 'Love each other' are not a simple suggestion or even an exhortation; they are a command. How can Christians best obey this command? In your experience, and from what you know of the Church worldwide, how do you think this command is being obeyed?
3. Read carefully and reflectively the well-known words of 1 Corinthians 13:4–7. Maybe you could even learn these verses by heart.

Light to live by

'Let there be love shared among us.'⁷ Use the description of love in 1 Corinthians 13:4–7 as a basis for your prayer. Ask God to enable you to love in such a way. Pray for your own church, that the members would truly love each another. Pray in the same way for the Church worldwide.

Lord, the light of Your love is shining,
in the midst of the darkness, shining:
Jesus, Light of the world, shine upon us;
set us free by the truth You now bring us –
shine on me, shine on me.

Shine, Jesus, shine,
fill this land with the Father's glory;
blaze Spirit, blaze,
Set our hearts on fire.
Flow, river, flow,
flood the nations with grace and mercy;
send forth Your word, Lord,
and let there be light!

Graham Kendrick © 1988 Make Way Music.
www.grahamkendrick.co.uk[8]

28 Dec

Children of light

Light for your path

For you were once darkness, but now you are light in the
Lord. Live as children of light (for the fruit of the light consists
in all goodness, righteousness and truth) and find out what
pleases the Lord. Have nothing to do with the fruitless deeds
of darkness, but rather expose them. For it is shameful even
to mention what the disobedient do in secret. But everything
exposed by the light becomes visible, for it is light that makes
everything visible. This is why it is said:

'Wake up, O sleeper,
   rise from the dead,
and Christ will shine on you.'

Ephesians 5:8–14

In this letter to the church at Ephesus, Paul refers to the believers as
having had dark lives. He doesn't just say that they had been living
in a dark world, but that they themselves were dark. He says, 'You
were once darkness,' ('representing ignorance, error and evil'[9]). Then
he goes on to say, '... but now ...' And we discover that the very
opposite is true. 'But now you are light' ('representing truth and
righteousness'[10]). How wonderful! 'You are light in the Lord,' he says.

They are illumined by Christ. They are in the light and the light is in them. 'The light metaphor speaks vividly of Christian openness and transparency, of living joyfully in the presence of Christ, with nothing to hide or fear.'[11] Paul exhorts them to live accordingly, so as to radiate the light: 'Live as children of light ...' And he even spells out what that means in practice. He talks about 'the fruit of the light' and contrasts it with 'the fruitless deeds of darkness'. 'The fruit of the light,' he says, 'consists in all goodness, righteousness and truth ...' We have a responsibility to live in a way that pleases the Lord. At the same time, we must 'have nothing to do with the fruitless deeds of darkness'. Christians living in the light will in fact show up the 'deeds of darkness' for what they are. As these deeds are exposed, so the perpetrators have the opportunity of turning to the light. They are exhorted to 'wake up' in the light of Christ as a new day dawns.

Shedding light

The year 2009 was a key year for Geneva and not only for Geneva but also for anywhere in the world where the influence of the Reformation has been felt. For 2009 marked the 500th anniversary of the birth of John Calvin, a prime example of one of those 'children of light' mentioned by Paul in today's text. Theologians and Christian historians from all over the world gathered in Geneva to give thanks for Calvin's life. Conferences and different celebrations were organised in his memory. Born in 1509 in Noyon, France, the young Calvin, a brilliant student, later recognised what he called his blindness and his need to be illuminated by God. Passing through Geneva, with no intention of staying there, he was detained by William Farel, who himself burned with a wonderful evangelistic zeal and who saw in Calvin the potential for causing God's light to shine into the city and so dispel the darkness and gloom that had gathered there. Calvin himself had 'une vision lumineuse' – 'a bright vision' – of a new society. The reforms he brought about were all carried out with the aim of bringing glory to God. On Calvin's death in Geneva in 1564, another reformer, Beza, remarked that the greatest light that had ever existed in this world for leading the Church of God had been taken up to heaven. Now Geneva's motto, inscribed at the back of 'the Reformers' Wall' is 'Post tenebras lux' ('after the darkness light').

Let your light shine

1. What would you say that darkness and light represent?
2. What does it mean in practice to 'live as children of light'?
3. What is your attitude to those still living in the darkness?

Light to live by

Pray for those in the world who are still 'darkness', those who perpetrate evil, who plan terrorist attacks, who abuse children, who cheat and steal and murder. Pray that those who live as children of light will expose these wicked deeds and that those who are responsible will be convicted of their sin and will be drawn into the light.

1. Philip E. Hughes, *Commentary on the Second Epistle to the Corinthians* (Grand Rapids, Michigan: Eerdmans, 1962) p.133.
2. Francis Wright Beare, *The First Epistle of Peter* (Oxford: Blackwell, 1947) p.106.
3. Graham Kendrick, 'Meekness and majesty' (Make Way Music, 1986).
4. David Jackman, *The Message of John's Letters* (Leicester: IVP, 1988) p.26.
5. Ibid., p.30.
6. John R.W. Stott, *The Letters of John*, Revised Edition (Leicester: IVP, 1995) pp.98–99.
7. Dave Bilbrough, 'Let there be love shared among us' (Kingsway Thankyou Music, 1979).
8. Extract from 'Shine, Jesus, shine' used with permission.
9. John R.W. Stott, *God's New Society* (Leicester: IVP, 1979) p.199.
10. Ibid., p.199.
11. Ibid., p.199.

No More Night

Having looked at parts of the Old Testament, the Gospels and brief extracts from some of the New Testament letters, we now come to the last book of the Bible, the book of Revelation. Written by the apostle John, in exile on the island of Patmos (Rev. 1:9), this book contains a good deal of strange prophetic symbolism. For that reason it is not easy to understand. John writes of eternal realities which are beyond our experience. However, it is clear that when Jesus comes again, the devil will be defeated and night will give way to day; darkness will give way to light. John has a vision of the risen glorified Christ: 'His head and hair were white like wool, as white as snow, and his eyes were like blazing fire. His feet were like bronze glowing in a furnace, and his voice was like the sound of rushing waters ... His face was like the sun shining in all its brilliance' (Rev. 1:14–16). In a similar vision Ezekiel saw the Lord surrounded by 'brilliant light'. 'Like the appearance of a rainbow in the clouds on a rainy day, so was the radiance around him' (Ezek. 1:27–28). Writing to the Thessalonians, Paul tells them to be prepared: 'But you, brothers, are not in darkness so that this day should surprise you like a thief. You are all sons of the light and

sons of the day. We do not belong to the night or to the darkness'
(1 Thess. 5:4–5). In the verses that we have chosen from the book
of Revelation – all from the last two chapters – the glory of God
shines forth, and we can rejoice that 'There will be no more night'
(Rev. 22:5).

A precious jewel

Light for your path

> One of the seven angels ... came and said to me, 'Come, I will
> show you the bride, the wife of the Lamb.' And he ... showed
> me the Holy City, Jerusalem, coming down out of heaven from
> God. It shone with the glory of God, and its brilliance was like
> that of a very precious jewel, like a jasper, clear as crystal.
>
> Revelation 21:9–11

In these verses John describes a vision that he saw, a vision of
'the Holy City, Jerusalem', which he also describes as 'the bride,
the wife of the Lamb'. The city was not built by human hands. We
often talk of constructions as 'going up'. However, this city 'came
down' from heaven to earth. It was obviously from God. John gives
a beautiful description of it: 'It shone with the glory of God'. The
city is illuminated, and its light comes from God, who is present.
It shines like a very precious stone. It is bright and it sparkles;
it is 'clear as crystal'. This is the fulfilment of Isaiah's prophecy:
'Arise, shine, for your light has come, and the glory of the LORD
rises upon you ... Nations will come to your light, and kings to the
brightness of your dawn ... The sun will no more be your light by
day, nor will the brightness of the moon shine on you, for the LORD
will be your everlasting light, and your God will be your glory'
(Isa. 60:1,3,19).

Shedding light

As we remarked in the introduction to this week's studies, there
is much symbolism in the book of Revelation. At the beginning
of chapter 21 John refers to this same vision of 'the Holy City, the

new Jerusalem' as symbolising 'a bride beautifully dressed for her husband' (v.2). It would seem that he refers to the Church, which is sometimes called the Bride of Christ, or – as in today's passage – 'the wife of the Lamb'. Jesus is 'the Lamb of God, who takes away the sin of the world' (John 1:29). So this beautifully illuminated city is in fact the Church. And the Church – just like a city – is made up of people. Fellowship and togetherness are implicit in John's description. In this vision of the radiant Church everything is perfect. We shall truly be one in Christ and bring glory to Him.

Let your light shine
1. As we look forward to our place in the kingdom of heaven, we cannot really imagine what it will be like. The Bible gives us a glimpse – often symbolic – here and there, but the reality surely goes a long way beyond our imagination or experience. Meditate on what today's passage describes symbolically. What aspect of 'the Holy City' appeals to you most?
2. In our introduction to this week's readings, we quoted from Paul's first letter to the Thessalonians. Read the whole of the relevant passage: 1 Thessalonians 4:13–5:11. Twice in this passage Paul tells the believers to encourage each other (4:18 and 5:11). How do you think we can best 'encourage one another and build each other up'?

Light to live by
Thank You, Lord, that one day You are coming back. And we will be with You for ever. Thank You for this picture we have in Your Word of the Holy City illuminated by Your presence.

30 Dec

The Lamb is its lamp

Light for your path

The city does not need the sun or the moon to shine on it, for the glory of God gives it light, and the Lamb is its lamp. The nations will walk by its light, and the kings of the earth will

bring their splendour into it. On no day will its gates ever be
shut, for there will be no night there.

Revelation 21:23–25

What a picture! The city needs no source of external light, not even
that of the sun or the moon, for it is lit up from within. It is filled
with the presence of God. It is His glory that illuminates it. And His
light shines constantly. There is no darkness. Night will never fall.
John tells us that 'the Lamb is its lamp'. Splendour radiates from the
presence of God and the Lamb. As we mentioned yesterday, 'the
Lamb' is Jesus. And we know that He and the Father are one (see
John 10:30). It is because 'he was led like a lamb to the slaughter'
(Isa. 53:7), that everyone has the opportunity of turning to Him
for salvation. Referring to the city, John specifies that 'The nations
will walk by its light'. By 'nations' he means all those – whatever
their origin – who have accepted Christ as Saviour. They will be
active: they 'will walk'. 'By their walk is meant their entire life and
conversation, all their activity, and that too, in relation to God.'[1] At
the same time, 'the kings of the earth will bring their splendour into
it'. The city is open to all of God's children, 'those whose names are
written in the Lamb's book of life' (Rev. 21:27).

Shedding light

These days people have double locks on their doors, as well as bolts
and electronic burglar alarms. Who would ever think of going to bed
without locking up? Security measures are essential. But in 'the Holy
City' there will be no need for all these precautions! No burglars,
no intruders, no enemies! There won't ever be any night anyway,
and the gates to the city will always stand open. Sin and evil will
have disappeared. Isaiah's prophecy that we referred to yesterday
says: 'Your gates will always stand open, they will never be shut ...'
(Isa. 60:11). Believers will be completely secure, lit up by the Lord's
presence in this radiant city.

Let your light shine

1. Read the full description of 'the Holy City, the new Jerusalem'
   in Revelation chapter 21. Who will inhabit this city? Who will be
   excluded from it? Why?

2. The vision of this symbolic city, as John describes it, is that of an enormous cube of outstanding beauty. What do you think is the key element in his description?

Light to live by

If you know that your name is 'written in the Lamb's book of life', rejoice and praise the Lord for the salvation you have in Him. Thank Him that you will spend eternity in His presence, where 'There will be no more death or mourning or crying or pain' (Rev. 21:4). Keep praying for those you know who have not yet put their trust in Christ. Ask God to draw them to Himself and save them.

---

31 Dec

God gives light

Light for your path

> There will be no more night. They will not need the light of a lamp or the light of the sun, for the Lord God will give them light … 'I, Jesus … am … the bright Morning Star.'
>
> Rev. 22:5,16

John obviously wants his readers to grasp what he is saying, so he repeats himself and underlines the fact that in heaven 'there will be no more night.' This confirms Zechariah's prophecy: 'It will be a unique day, without daytime or night-time – a day known to the LORD. When evening comes, there will be light' (Zech. 14:7). God gives the light, because God *is* light. As one commentator says, 'In the New Jerusalem God is ever present, and his glory makes unnecessary all other sources of light.'[2] We shall be with God, and He will be with us, and He will give us light.

The main part of Revelation chapter 22 – from verse 6 to the end of the chapter – is basically an epilogue. We are reminded that Jesus is coming again and that He is 'coming soon' (vv.12,20). He is 'the bright Morning Star', heralding a new day. The long night of darkness will soon be at an end. The new day is dawning.

Shedding light

During the day, even when the sun is obscured by the clouds a certain amount of light shines through. When evening comes, particularly in winter when the days are short, we need some form of artificial lighting in the streets and in our homes. Street lamps illuminate the roads and we have lights in our houses. Most of us rely on electricity. Recent severe storms in different parts of France left many homes without electricity for several weeks. Candles and wood fires were a poor substitute for the brighter electric lights. When the new day dawns, particularly if the sun shines, there is no further need for artificial lighting.

How good to know that Jesus is 'the bright Morning Star'! What hope and joy that gives us! We know that one day all the darkness and suffering of this earth will be a thing of the past. God's purposes will all be fulfilled. A new day is dawning, illuminated by God's presence, and 'there will be no more night'.

A couple of weeks ago we quoted that lovely hymn by Philip Bliss – 'The light of the world is Jesus.' The last verse is really a summary of John's teaching in these final chapters of Revelation:

No need of the sunlight in heaven, we're told;
The Light of that world is Jesus;
The Lamb is the Light in the City of Gold,
The Light of that world is Jesus.

P.P. Bliss (1838–1876)

Let your light shine

1. I suggest you read the whole of the epilogue (Rev. 22:6–21). How do you react to these final words of the apostle John?
2. What does it mean to you personally to know that Jesus is 'the bright Morning Star'?
3. How might this future hope of glory influence the way you live now? (The apostle Peter gives some suggestions. See 1 Peter 4:7–11.)

Light to live by

Thank You, Lord, for revealing to us something of the wonder and the glory of heaven. Our finite minds cannot take it all in. It is still beyond our experience. But we rejoice to know that one day we will be in Your presence. We will see You face to face. In the meantime we want to live for You in this world where You have placed us. We want to shine as lights for You. We bow before You and worship You. Be glorified, Lord. 'Amen. Come, Lord Jesus' (Rev. 22:20).

1. Herman Hoeksema, *Behold He Cometh, An exposition of the Book of Revelation* (Grand Rapids, Michigan: Reformed Free Publishing Association, 1969) p.703.
2. Robert H. Mounce, *The Book of Revelation* (London: Marshall, Morgan & Scott, 1977) p.388.

National Distributors

UK: (and countries not listed below)
CWR, Waverley Abbey House, Waverley Lane, Farnham, Surrey GU9 8EP.
Tel: (01252) 784700 Outside UK (44) 1252 784700

AUSTRALIA: CMC Australasia, PO Box 519, Belmont, Victoria 3216.
Tel: (03) 5241 3288 Fax: (03) 5241 3290

CANADA: David C Cook Distribution Canada, PO Box 98, 55 Woodslee Avenue, Paris, Ontario N3L 3E5.
Tel: 1800 263 2664

GHANA: Challenge Enterprises of Ghana, PO Box 5723, Accra.
Tel: (021) 222437/223249 Fax: (021) 226227

HONG KONG: Cross Communications Ltd, 1/F, 562A Nathan Road, Kowloon.
Tel: 2780 1188 Fax: 2770 6229

INDIA: Crystal Communications, 10-3-18/4/1, East Marredpalli, Secunderabad – 500026, Andhra Pradesh.
Tel/Fax: (040) 27737145

KENYA: Keswick Books and Gifts Ltd, PO Box 10242–00400, Nairobi.
Tel: (254) 20 312639/3870128

MALAYSIA: Salvation Book Centre (M) Sdn Bhd, 23 Jalan SS 2/64, 47300 Petaling Jaya, Selangor.
Tel: (03) 78766411/78766797 Fax: (03) 78757066/78756360

Canaanland, No. 25 Jalan PJU 1A/41B, NZX Commercial Centre, Ara Jaya, 47301 Petaling Jaya, Selangor.
Tel: (03) 7885 0540/1/2 Fax: (03) 7885 0545

NEW ZEALAND: CMC Australasia, PO Box 303298, North Harbour, Auckland 0751.
Tel: 0800 449 408 Fax: 0800 449 049

NIGERIA: FBFM, Helen Baugh House, 96 St Finbarr's College Road, Akoka, Lagos.
Tel: (01) 7747429/4700218/825775/827264

PHILIPPINES: OMF Literature Inc, 776 Boni Avenue, Mandaluyong City.
Tel: (02) 531 2183 Fax: (02) 531 1960

SINGAPORE: Alby Commercial Enterprises Pte Ltd, 95 Kallang Avenue #04-00, AIS Industrial Building, 339420.
Tel: (65) 629 27238 Fax: (65) 629 27235

SOUTH AFRICA: Struik Christian Books, 80 MacKenzie Street, PO Box 1144, Cape Town 8000.
Tel: (021) 462 4360 Fax: (021) 461 3612

SRI LANKA: Christombu Publications (Pvt) Ltd, Bartleet House, 65 Braybrooke Place, Colombo 2.
Tel: (9411) 2421073/2447665

USA: David C Cook Distribution Canada, PO Box 98, 55 Woodslee Avenue, Paris, Ontario N3L 3E5, Canada.
Tel: 1800 263 2664

ZIMBABWE: Word of Life Books (Pvt) Ltd, Christian Media Centre, 8 Aberdeen Road, Avondale, PO Box A480
Avondale, Harare.
Tel: (04) 333355 or 091301188

For email addresses, visit the CWR website: www.cwr.org.uk

CWR is a Registered Charity - Number 294387

CWR is a Limited Company registered in England - Registration Number 1990308

Get a deeper understanding of Scripture

Cover to Cover Every Day daily Bible-reading notes provide thought-provoking study of Bible books, stories and characters. They feature:

- A short, in-depth Bible study every day
- A rolling five-year curriculum covering every book of the Bible
- Bible references and a prayer for each day
- Contributions from well-known authors including R.T. Kendall, Jeff Lucas, Joel Edwards and Philip Greenslade.

Over a five-year period you will be taken through each book of the Bible. Every issue includes contributions from two different authors.

Cover to Cover Every Day
daily Bible-reading notes by various authors
170x120mm booklet – six issues per year published bimonthly
£13.80 for a 1-year subscription (UK)
£2.49 each (exc P&P) for individual issues

Journey through the Bible, as it happened, in a year

Your confidence in the Bible will increase as you see how it forms a single, comprehensive story across the centuries. This thrilling voyage of discovery through God's Word includes:

- Charts, maps, illustrations and diagrams that will enhance your understanding of the Bible's big story and biblical times
- A timeline across each page to keep every event in context for you
- Devotional thoughts to help you apply each day's reading
- The full text of the flowing, contemporary Holman Christian Standard translation, divided into manageable daily portions in chronological order.

Reference Book of the Year 2008 – UK Christian Booksellers

Cover to Cover Complete
by Selwyn Hughes and Trevor J. Partridge
1,632-page hardback
ISBN: 978-1-85345-433-2
Only £19.99

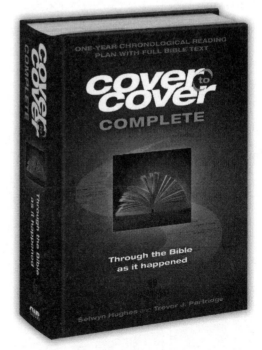